The Art
of a
Genuine Apology

The Art
of a
Genuine Apology

Bringing healing to your most significant relationships

ANDREW L. BLACKWOOD

Edited by Real Success Solutions Group

Cover design courtesy of Mark Anthoney Blackwood

NEXUS AND SERENITY PUBLISHING
TORONTO, CANADA

Printed in Canada
First Printing, August 2017
ISBN 978-1-7750548-0-1

Nexus And Serenity Publishing, a division of Nexus And Serenity
502-30 Gillingham Drive, Suite 522
Brampton ON, L6X 4P8
CANADA

nexusandserenity.coachdrew.ca

Dedicated to all who desire to Learn, Heal and Grow.

CONTENTS

Acknowledgments

God, I am grateful for every opportunity to learn, heal, and grow. I consider myself the richest man in the world because of the wonderful and wise people you have placed in my life. I want to share the wisdom I receive with everyone.

To my loving, patient, understanding and supportive wife, Adene, I appreciate your unwavering support of me and your willingness to share our time with others. Without your constant belief in me, your feedback and your active involvement in this process, I would not have been able to accomplish all that I have. I love you and thank God for you.

To my lovely daughters, Anya and Aileen, thank you for helping me venture beyond theory into practice in every area of my life.

To my artistic, graphically and conceptually gifted brother, seeing you pursue your passion inspires me more than you know. Thank you for believing in me, loving me and supporting me the way you do!

To my sisters, Tamaira and Samantha, thank you for always caring enough to see beyond my flaws and love me anyway! Your constant prayers make a difference!

Mom and Dad, without your sacrifices and your unending commitment to God and to your children I would not be the man that I am today!

Pastor Dwight Richards, Romeo Frank, Tamaira Blackwood and my darling wife, your feedback, questions and suggestions have made this book so much more valuable. Thank you for your help and support throughout this process!

To my closest friends, Mentors and treasured Professors, I know a cursory mention of our many conversations and your contributions to my life over the years will not do you justice, but I want it to be canonized. I would not be the me I am without all of you.

To Janice James-Brown, you have taken my initial attempt at writing about this worthwhile topic and helped me turn it into something a larger audience can understand and make use of. Thank you!

To all of the people who have helped to shape my life, including my clients, thank you for your willingness to share your stories with me and entrusting me with your hearts. I learn every day with and from you. You have given me more than you will ever know, and for that, I remain forever grateful.

Special Note
from the Author

When you whittle it all down, the heart of Counselling is about one simple act, listening. The stories I am privileged to hear, and help people rewrite, often entail moments of pain and sheer horror. People often ask me, "How do you do what you do? How do you turn it off and leave work at work? The truth is, I don't turn it off. The stories people share with me stay with me. In fact, they move me to reflect beyond individual trauma in the city and place I call home to the worldwide occurrences of rape, human trafficking and genocide. It's real. It's dark. And, it's devastating.

As much as we try to avoid hearing it, these happenings give voice to the reality of an evil that is both spiritual and systemic. Whether we are its victims directly or tune it out for as long as we can, it is shaping our societies and permeating our souls. I don't want to scare you with such a dark announcement at the outset of this work, however, hearing about harmful practices that seep into the fabric of people's lives and become established norms of families, cultures and countries around the globe is the overarching reason for this book, to change the hurtful patterns and practices in our world. I know it sounds ridiculous, one person changing the world, however, despite how powerless we may feel in the face of inhumane and spiritually damning occurrences, it is critical to note that horrific acts are always expressed through the choices of individuals. The gift of choice so often used to hurt can also be used to heal. We can choose to listen. We can choose to put the needs of others before our own. We can choose to be agents of healing for ourselves and others. Having witnessed fort like emotional walls, built from years of pain, give way to the healing power of forgiveness, acceptance and love, I've grown confident in the opportunities for us all to choose to respond to life's scariest, darkest and most hurtful moments with wisdom, courage and compassion. We can choose to heal, to help, to forgive, to apologize, to be reconciled.

More stabilizing than many years of counselling experience and spiritual reflection, is a daily heart-reviving journey with Jesus that has, and continues to shape my worldview. It inspires me, gives me direction and fills me with hope. I don't know how others do it, but that's how I take the realities of this world and the stories of others home with me without getting lost in the dark, so to speak.

So, within the pages that follow you might catch glimpses of the faith and spirituality that makes me, me. I proudly acknowledge that the information and wisdom contained within this book flow out of years spent with, and learning from, people of differing ages, backgrounds and perspectives. *The Art of a Genuine Apology* is written for everyone and anyone with a particular need; the need to address relational hurt, the hurts endured by those you love as well as the hurts you've caused them.

My hope and prayer is that it will bring healing to your life, your relationships and our world. I choose to believe that through mastering the art of a Genuine Apology, truly caring for those closest to us, we can address hurt all around the world and overcome evil with good!

Foreword

By Dr. John Hull

Lead Pastor of Eastside Baptist Church, Marietta, GA, USA

I know little of the sport of archery but I certainly admire the precision and skill required to hit a small target yards away. Do you realize that the concept behind archery is mentioned within the first chapters of the Bible? Not by name but the intention is certainly there. Satan eyed his target, Adam and Eve's flesh nature, and with pinpoint accuracy he nailed them. Sadly, he's still on his game today.

In his book, The Art of a Genuine Apology, Andrew Blackwood addresses one of Satan's prime targets in relationships - preventing reconciliation through genuine forgiveness. We are quick with an "I'm sorry" if necessary but offering a sincere apology that leads to healing is a communication skill that we either misunderstand or foolishly reject.

Andrew has a heart for reconciliation and practical solutions for the challenges in relationships. In his years of working as a Registered Psychotherapist he has seen the damage of words left unsaid.

I have had the privilege of interviewing Andrew on 100 Huntley Street multiple times. I found him to be not only knowledgeable and engaging but genuinely passionate about helping create an atmosphere in relationships where emotional and spiritual health can flourish. As you read this book you will find very practical, doable strategies for living out God's truth of restoration.

What impresses me most though is the man. Andrew lives in reality. He is practical. He is experienced. He is personable. And most of all Andrew is a gifted, dedicated servant fulfilling God's call to bring healing in people's lives and he does it very well. You might say he is right on target.

Preface

Can you imagine being in a relationship with someone who refuses to apologize when they have hurt you or someone else? What about being in a relationship with someone who believes they are always right? The truth is, many of you reading these words don't have to imagine, because this is your painful reality. It is for you, and countless others like you who have longed for, or longed to give genuine apologies for wrongs experienced or inflicted, that I embarked upon the journey of writing this book.

I imagine that some people might think, *"What's the big deal anyway? I don't need a book to tell me how to apologize."* Others may wonder, *"Is giving an apology worth all of this thought and attention?"* Well, the answer is, Yes! Yes, apologies, at least the ones I am writing about, are a big deal. Yes, many of us need some help in making apologies that matter. And, Yes, apologies, Genuine Apologies, are worth all the attention!

Speaking as a Psychotherapist and an experienced workshop facilitator who has spent many years listening to the painful experiences of others, I have an intimate knowledge of the healing that a Genuine Apology can bring. The tips, techniques and tools I offer in this book, and in my workshops about Genuine Apologies, have significantly changed the course of many conversations and interactions to produce amazing outcomes. I have had the distinct honour of watching the cold, angry and even distant relationships of many of the people I have worked with become fruitful and loving because they were open to receiving guidance and willing to try something a little different. I have seen old hurts healed and patterns of conflict and misunderstandings changed. I have witnessed pivotal moments of hurt and anger give way to expressions of understanding and appreciation. Interactions that would have turned into heated arguments instantly cooled and transformed into loving exchanges.

By offering insight to those who have been hurt by withheld apologies, poorly delivered apologies and insincere apologies, I hope to stimulate emotional healing and help anyone who earnestly desires to improve their most significant relationships. Through thoughtful consideration, self-reflection and the application of the principles shared in this book, I believe you can effectively respond to the hurtful interactions between you and those you care about.

Ultimately, these strategies and principles teach people how to avoid common mistakes and bring clarity to those who want to give and receive Genuine Apologies.

Today, in this moment, I encourage you to be open and present as you read this book.

Through reading this book and practicing the art of a Genuine Apology I believe you will experience the joy of bringing healing to your most significant relationships. If you're tired of encounters that fall short of the healing and forgiveness you desire and are ready to take steps towards change, then this book is for you.

Enjoy!

About this book and how to use it

Some people may say, "You don't need a book on how to apologize, just say sorry and mean it." Unfortunately, my experience, as well as the experiences shared with me by others attests to the fact that, quite often, simply saying sorry and meaning it is not good enough! That's one of the major reasons why I decided to write this book. In fact, this book is about so much more than just "making an apology."

The goal of this book is to offer insight, increase your awareness and understanding and invite change; change in the way you view situations, respond when you hurt others, or react when hurt by others. While this book is filled with useful information, principles, strategies and wisdom acquired over more than a decade of working with individuals, couples and families, it is not meant to be a clinical intervention or a substitute for engaging in counselling. Rather, consider this book a resource, a guide on how to go about doing something very important that we all are expected to do, but haven't really been taught how to do well. So, you will not find numbers or statistics based on surveys or experiments. Instead, what you will find within these pages are strategies and principles to help you understand what others need from you in an apology and assist you with helping others improve the apologies they offer to you.

This book is designed to do three important things: share information, promote reflection and encourage intentional action. While these three objectives are present throughout this work, the layout of this book also features these three objectives building on each other in distinct segments. Chapters 1 through 4 comprise the first segment where we explore different kinds of apologies and their foundational components, the nuts and bolts, if you will.

Chapter 5 moves us to the next segment, where we begin to appreciate the attention to detail and the effort involved in developing the art of what I call a Genuine Apology. Chapter 6 explores its complex nature and delves into the essential elements that make a Genuine Apology so powerful, setting it apart from all other apologies. Chapter 7 continues to prepare you, endeavouring to increase awareness about the differences between an apology, forgiveness and reconciliation. Chapters 8 and 9 round out this second segment by highlighting things to avoid, as well as anticipate, when giving and receiving a Genuine Apology.

The final segment of this book, chapters 10

through 15, pulls all the parts and pieces together to help you with the delivery. These chapters clearly layout the 4 steps to offering a Genuine Apology and incorporate all of the elements discussed throughout this book so that you'll be able to see how everything comes together to create the Masterpiece, hereby known as the Genuine Apology.

To help you focus in on some of the key concepts being discussed throughout the journey, I have incorporated a few stories. And, at the close of many of the chapters you'll find questions and strategies intentionally noted as "for your consideration", an invitation for you to pause, reflect and truly consider.

In order to get the most out of this book, active exploration and open-hearted participation is required. I encourage you to let your guard down and be honest with yourself. Make notes, highlight meaningful sections and keep a journal or notebook handy for additional questions, topics or memories that come to mind.

Finally, be sure to make use of each step to create your unique plan so that this information moves beyond the pages of this book and into your life where it will achieve the ultimate purpose of bringing healing to your most significant relationships.

Introduction

Awareness is an amazing thing!

Near the end of my graduate studies in 2004, I was a student facilitator in a program for offenders as part of my counselling internship. Sitting in a room each Wednesday night for 6 months with sixteen to twenty-five men, most of them charged with abusing their intimate partners, made me realize that emotional awareness, thoughtfulness and compassion are gifts that many people have never unwrapped. It also gifted me with the awareness that I had taken many things for granted. The growth this experience provided was so valuable that I returned later in my career for a number of years to help others experience and continue their growth.

Of the years I co-facilitated the program only one brave man came voluntarily to learn and receive support in developing the skills necessary to stop his hurtful and destructive behavior. The rest of the men I met in that program were ordered to attend or face harsher consequences ranging from fines to imprisonment. With the exception of this one man, they were either unaware, or unwilling at that point, to take ownership of the choices that lead to this place of exposed confinement. Can you imagine being

1

forced to go to a place where you are made to recite and relive hurtful, destructive behaviors? Well, these men were called to account for actions that increased the havoc, discord and distrust in their relationships and acknowledge the impact upon their partners and in some cases, their children.

I imagine that everyone has experienced regret at some point in their lives, but for many of these men, this place of consequence produced palpable regret. I mean you could feel the tension and even sorrow in the room, yet, opening themselves up to any experience of empathy and remorse remained undesirable and unwelcome. In fact, during our discussions most of them exhibited unsettling discomfort, shifted in their seats, clenched their jaws and were unwilling to express remorse and empathy to the people they had hurt. Worse than those reactions was the dismissive, laid back laissez faire disposition worn by some as if no ill had transpired.

Regardless of their presentation, these men were nowhere close to being ready to offer an apology of any kind. I often walked away from these chilling and frustrating moments reflecting on how accurately empathy and remorse indicate a deep awareness of our impact on others. I now know that without this deep awareness, it is impossible to experience genuine and lasting change.

Like the men from that Wednesday night group, many people live without a deep awareness of their impact on others, remaining focused on their intentions citing things like, "It wasn't my intention for him/her to think that" or "I didn't mean for this to happen." Along with this misdirected focus on intentions is the assumption that moving past hurt will be easy and that things will automatically change. That season of life taught me this important lesson, changes that pave the way for deep healing are never automatic.

As challenging as this experience was for me, it was a catalyst for change and growth in my own life. Yes, I grew as a professional, but more importantly, I grew as a man. Each and every week I was reminded of the painful places that we, as wonderfully flawed human beings, can find ourselves when the many principles about relationships contained within this book are not observed. I became more aware of my emotions and the fact that making changes to the way we live, communicate and relate to others is challenging, but there is absolutely no other way to grow and bring healing to our most significant relationships!

So, just in case you were more focused on seeing changes in others and receiving a Genuine Apology for yourself, please don't overlook the value of being changed and altering the way you view situations, the way you respond to hurtful moments and the way you offer a Genuine Apology. This book is a guide for experiencing change within yourself as well as the relationships you are a part of. Always remember, there's no better way to offer guidance than being an experienced and competent guide.

Chapter One

What is an apology?

Have you ever traveled on the subway of a major city? They are fast-paced, crowded environments, filled with the bustling sounds of people going about their lives. We can imagine that most of these people may never see each other again, yet, on any given day one can hear the words, "I'm sorry", "I'm sorry", "I'm sorry" voiced many times over. Whether a stranger bumps into you on the train, you awkwardly sidestep someone on a sidewalk or pass through a line at a supermarket, these two words are used over and over again to acknowledge one's actions that have impacted another, usually causing some form of inconvenience. Invariably, when we think of an apology, it involves these two words.

While our daily interactions have made the use of these words commonplace, their meaning and impact can also vary drastically depending on the situation.

We can be liberal, offering them superficially to strangers and acquaintances as in the instances mentioned above or these same two words, offered to those we are in close relationships with, can form an entire phrase, end an argument or be the precursor to a cataclysmic fight.

Our recognition of the wide range of meaning and impact of apologies lends to acknowledging our life-long history with apologies. Whenever I offer a workshop on the art of a Genuine Apology I ask participants to try to recall their earliest memories of an apology. Many describe scenarios of parents pushing them to apologize, believing they were doing the right thing. For me, my earliest memories of apologies still ring clearly in my ears: *"What?!?! Andrew, you did what?!?!?! Say sorry! No buts! Say sorry right now! Hug him and say you're sorry! Fix your face! I didn't raise you to be like that!"*

Taking creative license here, I can picture my brother standing in the background with a mischievous smirk on his face as I am being held to task. And you know what was the worst part?! I had no reason to apologize. I didn't start it. He deserved it! It wasn't even my fault and I was being forced to apologize (at least that's how I remember most of my childhood conflicts with my brother). I know I am not the only one who bares these childhood scars. I witnessed this unjust scene in the lives of friends and family members many *many* times. I can still picture the real guilty party smiling with great satisfaction knowing they've won.

Truth be told, this kind of early education around apologies leaves many children feeling unsure, unprepared and ill-equipped to effectively navigate challenging relational situations. As sad as this is, the real tragedy is revealed when you fast forward twenty, thirty and even forty years on only to find the same dynamic birthed in childhood; adults apologizing to end an argument, avoid conflict, meet some sort of religious standard or relieve themselves of guilt. At the other end of the spectrum are those determined to win at all costs, refusing to back down or give in and would sooner die than say, "I am sorry".

Whether we find ourselves withholding apologies or giving them under duress, I believe we can all agree that at the very least, an apology is meant to address some sort of wrongdoing and expresses some amount of regret connected to negatively impacting another. Yet, even with this consensus, actually giving and receiving apologies remains difficult for many. While most of us are adept at offering casual apologies to strangers, the attempts at apologizing to those that matter the most to us fall short of being the kind of apologies people desire to receive. Whether a common apology is offered or the "right" phrases are pried from one's lips, they barely make it beyond expressions of regret and do more harm than good because they lack depth and meaning.

Having met with many unhappy, frustrated, unfulfilled people, I have discovered that the absence of giving and receiving meaningful apologies eventually leads to distance, bitterness and stagnation in relationships. Perhaps, like most of the workshop participants or many reading this book, you may not remember ever receiving or witnessing meaningful and effective apologies, but I don't want you to move ahead without first looking back. Skipping this step would be a terrible mistake. Please don't overlook the significance of absence. A brief acknowledgement of not having witnessed healthy apologies oversimplifies the reality that not only have we all learned from what was done but was left *un*done.

In my estimation, states of relational ill-health due to the indifference and even disdain toward apologies can be traced right back to our childhood days. Our early life experiences can inform our apologies and dictate the degree of hurt or healing experienced in our interactions. Without reflecting on our histories with poor experiences of desired, requested, offered or withheld apologies we can remain unsure about how to navigate critical moments. If we continue to choose not to reflect we, like the men in the group I shared of earlier, will remain unaware of the very things that can truly set us free.

The unvarnished truth? No matter which end of this spectrum, giving reluctantly or withholding indefinitely, the unexamined learning dating back to childhood interactions has left many individuals scarred, scared and unprepared for the give and take that apologies in healthy relationships demand. My aim is to help you move away from inadequate apologies and learn how to give and receive apologies that have depth and meaning; bringing new life and healing to your most significant relationships.

So now you are probably thinking (at least I hope you are) about the apologies you have offered. Did you really want to give them? Were they superficial? Did they actually express regret? Most importantly, were they actually meaningful? If you're unsure, there's no need to worry. We're about to walk through what makes an apology meaningful, but before we do, let's examine some of our individual practices and experiences of apologies by completing the Apology Quiz found on the next page.

The Apology Quiz

The apology quiz is a series of questions compiled to help you think about your current beliefs and practices related to giving and receiving apologies. Be sure to take the time to consider each question and your answer thoroughly.

1. Do you believe someone owes you an apology? .... Y/N

2. Are you tired of hearing apologies from the same person? .... Y/N

3. Are you finding it hard to accept a particular person's apology? .... Y/N

4. If you answered yes to the question above, do you know why? .... Y/N

5. Do you find it hard to admit when you're wrong? .... Y/N

6. Do you owe someone an apology? .... Y/N

7. Do you find it difficult to apologize even when you know you're wrong? .... Y/N

8. Have you ever apologized for something you were not responsible for? .... Y/N

9. Do you tend to apologize even when you are not responsible? .... Y/N

10. Have you ever felt skeptical about the sincerity of someone's apology? .... Y/N

11. Have you ever accepted an apology that you didn't think was sincere? .... Y/N

12. Are you able to determine if someone else's apology is sincere? .... Y/N

13. If you doubt someone's apology to be sincere, do you know what to do? .... Y/N

14. Do you expect people to accept your apologies right away? .... Y/N

15. Do you believe you have to accept someone's apology? .... Y/N

16. Is it your responsibility to teach others how to apologize to you? .... Y/N

17. Do you believe apologizing to children is important? .... Y/N

18. If you're a parent/guardian do you gladly apologize to your children? .... Y/N

If these questions have raised additional questions for you or brought to mind people or situations you want to address, this would be the perfect place to pause and write them down.

Now, let's move beyond the casual and common apology and explore the elements that add depth and meaning.

CHAPTER TWO

The Meaning-*full* Apology

Vastly different from the common apologies cited in the first chapter is what I have termed a meaning-full apology, an apology *full of meaning*.

Attributing meaning, interpreting situations and coming to conclusions about each and every experience is what we as human beings do. Therefore, each person decides what to make of *every* apology given to them. However, even though everyone may have their own definition of what is meaningful, there are two things I encourage people to look at in order to ensure their apologies are full of meaning, and they are: intention and sincerity.

A superficial glance at apologies could leave one thinking that intention and sincerity are both present and seeking the same result in every apology. However, that is not always the case and it is critical that we understand this distinction. Unlike a common apology, the purpose of a meaning-full apology is to bring intention and sincerity together to address the other person's hurt, make things right and heal the other person's pain. Let's take, for example, a person offering a well-deserved apology with the hope that they will be forgiven and that their apology will make the relationship better, leaving both parties *equally* happy in the end. While this may sound like a fair exchange, *I apologize and you apologize that way we both feel good when it's all over*, this approach actually detracts from effectively attending to the pain of the other person and presents great potential for the apology to be self-focused and even manipulative.

A meaning-full apology, on the other hand, will *always* seek the healing of the hurt party *first*, regardless of the outcome and impact on the relationship. In other words, the needs of the offended party are prioritized over those of the party offering the apology. Pause for a moment and take this in. Maybe I should say it again... A meaning-full apology, will always seek the healing of the hurt party first, *regardless of the outcome and impact on the relationship*. Can you tell that I am trying to bring as much attention as possible to the fact that considering the needs of another person is drastically different than prioritizing them? Whether or not an apology is accepted, one is given in return, or even if there is not a reuniting at the end of the apology, the primary aim of a meaning-full apology is to address the other person's hurt. Once again, a meaning-full apology requires bringing intention and sincerity together to focus on their healing before and above your own.

At this point you may well be wondering, *What about me???!!! Why should their hurt be prioritized over mine??? Andrew, is there nowhere in this process that the apology giver can experience benefits as well?* The answer is yes, but it cannot be at the expense of, or prioritized over, addressing the other person's hurt first. In many cases, apologies are withheld because both parties have experienced hurt. Some are even so bold as to say, "I won't apologize until you apologize to me, first." How often does that approach result in a heartfelt offering? Not very often.

For some strange reason, the race to offer an apology is one that people aim to come in second place. If you're not intentionally and sincerely seeking to win this race, it will cause you to lose in more ways than one. Remember my earlier statement that each person interprets and decides what to make of every apology? Well, in situations warranting a meaning-full apology, intentions and sincerity are scrutinized intensely. How the hearer feels after an apology has been given has a lot to do with the sincerity felt throughout the delivery. If there is even the slightest hint of reservation even a "well intended" apology will likely be misinterpreted and experienced as an additional offense. I want to bring more clarity to this by taking a closer look at intention and sincerity.

INTENTION

Intention can be defined as a person's reason, purpose, or overall desire. After more than a decade of providing counselling to individuals, couples and families, I have learned that good intentions don't always equal good outcomes. A true understanding of our intentions, as well as the intentions of others, can tell us a lot about an apology. The way to define the intention of one's apology is to zero in on the heart of *why* someone is apologizing (the reason) and *what* they hope their apology will accomplish (the purpose). We all have reasons for apologizing, however, very rarely do we stop to consider if the intentions behind our reasons are correctly focused. Perhaps it's offering an apology to avoid conflict, smooth things over and quickly get past a difficult moment. Or perhaps it is simply to avoid hurting someone.

These reasons may all have "good intentions", however good intentions alone are not good enough. A meaning-full apology requires intentions that are correctly focused. I use the phrase correctly focused intentions instead of good intentions because it highlights the difference between offerings focused on appeasing someone or avoiding conflict versus healing their hurt.

A lack of clarity around any aspect of intention can drastically affect the outcome of the interaction. Acquiring clarity about one's intentions is critical but not always easy. So, before even attempting to offer a meaning-full apology, asking and answering essential questions will help you clarify your intentions. I have shared some of these essential questions in the "for your consideration" section at the end of this chapter.

SINCERITY

When we search for a definition of the word sincerity we find a general statement that speaks to the quality of being free of pretense, deceit, or hypocrisy. In addition, words such as honesty, genuineness, truthfulness and integrity are all associated. In order for one's apology to be sincere, it must be free of reservations, dishonesty and manipulation of any kind. For the hearer to experience sincerity in an apology, honesty, truthfulness and genuineness must permeate it, from beginning to end.

To be sincere in one's apology is not always an easy feat. It requires thorough self-examination and a level of sacrifice that most people don't enjoy. At this level of apology, one is asked to hold up the mirror of self-reflection as they peer into their own motivations and desires. Here, emotions, thoughts and beliefs that one may not be ready, or even wish to face are often uncovered. This can be a place of extreme discomfort. However, no matter how challenging it may be to hold up the mirror of self-analysis, it is crucial to take this step to figure out whether or not your apology is sincere.

Why is this step so important? People who have been hurt, whether by you or someone else, are likely to be skeptical and even hypersensitive regarding sincerity. Whether or not we are aware of it, people look for sincerity in an apology or anticipate the absence of it. If your apology is not sincere, there is no reason to expect that the recipient will trust you or experience your apology as meaning-full. Without sincerity, the recipient will likely feel manipulated and angry. Let me remind you again that the purpose of a meaning-full apology is to bring intention and sincerity together to make things right and heal the *other* person's pain.

If you are really sincere and want someone to experience your apology as meaning-full, it is important to understand how sincerity and correctly focused intentions come together. It is equally important to be aware of the nuances that can quickly derail or effectively create a meaning-full apology. So, using the following story, let me take a moment to highlight the nuances of intention and sincerity and how they come together to create an apology full of meaning.

📖 The Struggle Is Real!

During one of my workshops, a participant, let's call her Julie, shared of struggling to apologize after a conversation that caused unintended hurt. The fact that she intended the exchange to be helpful stood in stark contrast to the other person's experience of it. As this was one of her most treasured and significant relationships, she was not only terribly sad because her friend was so hurt, she also felt obligated to offer an apology to soothe the hurt. On the other hand, she meant every word she said and still wanted her friend to hear the intended message. Her desire to apologize was coming from a good place, but she continually asked herself, *"Should I really be apologizing? Would I really mean it?"* I reminded Julie, and the group at large, that the paramount focus of a meaning-full apology is to bring healing to the other person's injury first.

As our discussion progressed, Julie recalled that the conversation with her friend was an intense one, with raised voices, harsh statements and unkind glares. She acknowledged feeling embarrassed and disappointed about how she handled herself and confessed that, if she could have a "do-over", she would communicate very differently, in a way that showed the love and respect she continues to have for her friend. But, despite Julie's recognition of her own disappointing behavior, she continued to feel uneasy and was struggling with what to do about the situation that had caused so much upheaval between her and her friend. Let's break this down, in order to gain clarity about the "why" or the reason for one's apology.

Understanding The 'Why'

Many people are invested in doing "the right thing" but are conflicted and hesitant regarding how to go about it, and for good reason. Be it the anticipation of a host of troubling emotions, uncertainty about who is truly at fault or fear of taking all the blame, this hesitation and the internal conflict are both common and understandable.

Have you ever had thoughts like these? *How can I get this to end? I just want to keep the peace... maybe I should just apologize. Apologizing is the right thing to do, isn't it?* If you have, it is important to know that even though being a peace-maker is a noble thing, apologizing and accepting the blame for something you did not do or apologizing simply because it is the right thing to do is a trap of good intentions. These may sound like meaning-full apologies but, these good intentioned acts, are actually not apologies at all. At best, this kind of apology is a well-disguised truce, a way to ease tension and move away from an upsetting or unpleasant moment. While many believe they are living up to a biblical standard or being the bigger person, they don't realize that accepting responsibility for another person's behavior renders their apology insincere and repeatedly doing so eventually leads to feelings of frustration and bitterness.

The truth is, even if the conflict and tension abates, the sense of relief and calm this course of action brings is temporary. In most cases, it also allows others to remain unaware of their problematic behavior and escape ownership of their actions, which in reality is a very *un*helpful thing. As I said before, good intentions don't always equal good outcomes. Remember, both sincerity and correctly focused intentions must be present for your apology to be meaning-full.

For anyone in situations such as these, a careful examination of your intentions will help you determine if an apology is not only appropriate, but something you actually want to offer as you seek to strengthen your most significant relationships. Our friend Julie was in this exact position. The more she acknowledged behaviors she was not proud of was the clearer her "why" or the reason for her apology became. She wanted to apologize for her tone of voice and the unkind glares because they didn't convey the love and admiration she has for her friend, yet Julie's struggle remained. When asked what her hesitation was about, Julie stated quite honestly, "I want to apologize, but I can't because I meant everything I said."

The closer Julie examined her reasons for apologizing as well as for withholding her apology, the more she learned about herself. At first she was embarrassed because she believed her hesitation was evidence that she has trouble acknowledging when she is wrong but in reality, she simply did not want to be disingenuous. Julie realized that, while an apology was deserved for the hurtful delivery of her thoughts about the issue, she did not wish to retract her statements at all and this was what her struggle was all about. The further she dug, the more she discovered.

As Julie reflected on her desire to be authentic and stand by her convictions similar incidents with other people over the years came to mind. In the midst of putting them all together she had an "ah-ha!" moment, "Wow! When I express my convictions to others I can come across as angry, judgmental and disrespectful. That's not my intention and that's definitely not how I want to be perceived".

As we continued to discuss the situation, Julie came to realize that her hopes of delivering a clear and important message were overshadowed by her strong feelings about the issue. Her intense conviction and passion snowballed into anger which was reflected in the tone of her delivery. This was the primary reason for her friend feeling hurt and disrespected. Julie came to understand that even when she feels strongly about something she always wants to communicate lovingly, and in this case, like many others in the past, she did not. Truly, her friend deserved an apology for the way she had spoken to her.

As Julie intentionally sought clarity around her "why" she learned something incredibly valuable about herself. Without this degree of self-examination leading to the awareness of the challenges of being a passionate person who values remaining resolute in her convictions, the recognition that her friend deserved an apology would not have been enough for her to overcome the struggle within. Resolving her internal conflict also helped to resolve the relational conflict as well. Meaning every word of her apology was of the utmost importance to Julie and, as noted earlier, sincerity permeating every word of the apology would also be essential for her friend to experience the apology as meaning-full as well. I believe it's critical for Julie and everyone else to be able to offer an apology without reservation. With that said, let's turn our attention to the "what", the purpose of her apology.

Tending To The 'What'

Having come to terms with the fact that her friend really deserved an apology, Julie could move on and devote her attention to exactly what she would say to ensure her apology was not only sincere but correctly focused. Julie could say something you may have heard a time or two before, "I am not sorry for what I said, but I am sorry for how I said it." While this might check the sincerity box, who would that "apology" be for? What would that accomplish? In all likelihood, this type of apology would be experienced as a statement that justified her hurtful expressions and not as an apology at all. Had Julie taken that route and given that type of apology, it would appease her conscience and reassert her right to defend her convictions but it would do nothing to address the hurt she caused. In reality, it would make the situation worse, leaving her friend more hurt than before, which is something that Julie obviously didn't want. But she didn't want to take back the words she said either, thus, the struggle continued.

Like Julie, many people feel conflicted and forced to take back what they've said because of how they've said it. As our discussion continued Julie appreciated the reminder that she wasn't the first nor would she be the last to wish for a do-over. The conversation also allowed Julie to understand that she did not need to retract her statements but rather apologize for her angry and judgmental tone of voice. An apology that addressed the judgmental tone was not only well-deserved but exactly what would allow her friend to remember the genuine respect and love they share despite a difference of opinion.

Both the reason for Julie's apology and the goal or purpose of her apology, to acknowledge where she went wrong and to restore the peace, harmony and respect in their relationship, became crystal clear. On top of that, without the need to retract the content of her statement Julie also felt relieved, free and happy about being able to sincerely offer a meaning-full apology, without reservation.

As we can see, intention and sincerity are multifaceted and will affect both the giver and the receiver in the process of offering an apology that is meaning-full. So, let's return to the question posed earlier. Is there a benefit for the giver of the apology as well as the receiver? Simply put, the answer is, Yes! As evidenced by Julie's experience, when an apology is sincere and correctly focused, one can apologize adequately and freely, without any reservations. As the one giving the correctly focused apology you can rest assured that you've done your best to address the hurt you've caused. And after this kind of apology there will be no need to take back what was said or wish for a "do-over".

We have used this chapter to build the foundation that sincerity and correctly focused intentions help an apology to be full of meaning for the recipient and has benefits for the giver as well. But this chapter would be incomplete without addressing a lurking, and often imperceptible danger: manipulation. Because of its prevalence and harm a discussion about apologies would be inadequate without preparing and equipping you to detect and disarm it.

MANIPULATION

Manipulation can be defined as the using, handling or controlling of something or someone for one's personal gain. When people come to me expressing anger and frustration about being manipulated, they often relay unbelievable stories of events and interactions laden with mixed messages and confusion. Without fail, they end up sharing about feeling guilty, blamed and responsible in some way and confused because they don't think they are responsible and have no idea of how it happens time and time again. This degree of upset about this emotionally taxing experience makes sense, but the inherent confusion also makes sense because the most effective forms of manipulation are subtly woven into our interactions without our being aware.

Really... How do you mean Andrew? Well, I'm glad you asked. Insincere apologies, apologies with self-serving agendas, apologies with add-ons, suggestive statements and statements in disguise are all forms of manipulation that many people use and experience without knowing it. Let's work through these types of manipulation one at a time.

Insincere Apologies

Whether one is willing to admit it or not, by its very nature, an insincere apology is a strategic and manipulative tactic. Here's a lighthearted example that I am sure many can relate to. Let's say you're in danger of missing your flight and your heart-pounding race to the airport is halted by lights and sirens. Yep, it's the perfect time for the Police to be doing their job. Instinctively, you say, "Officer, I am so sorry..." but are you really sorry for speeding? Nope. In fact, you wish they would forget about the hefty ticket you've earned and speed on ahead of you, blazing a trail through, around and even over traffic to get you on that plane. You might not think saying, "I am sorry" is an attempt to manipulate the Officer, but the Officer might see things a little differently.

Self-serving Agendas

Just as manipulative, but subtler than an insincere apology, is a sincere one combined with a self-serving agenda. "Honey, I was wrong for ignoring your calls today, I'm sorry. It wasn't a kind or mature thing to do... Let's not go to bed angry tonight?" While the words may sound great, the goal of this manipulative maneuver is to brush aside the offence and be completely pardoned despite how hurt the other person might still be feeling.

While not going to bed angry is a good thing, without giving the other person the opportunity to share their perspective or to address their hurt, the other person is encouraged to remain silent and covertly pushed to forgive right away. Furthermore, the well-coordinated timing of this request positions them as the one standing in the way of a peaceful night. Not only have their calls gone unanswered all day, but they have now been saddled with guilt and the challenge of snuggling in next to their "offender" for a good night's rest.

Apology Add-ons

Equally damaging, yet less covert than most self-serving agendas, are apology add-ons. That's when real expressions of guilt that involve berating yourself are tacked onto an apology, like this: "I'm so sorry, I feel so bad about what I did... I am so dumb... I'm such an idiot... I don't deserve someone like you." Whether it's your intention or not, and despite how much you mean every word gushing from the depths of your soul, an apology with this kind of add-on could leave someone feeling sad for you or even guilty when *they've* been hurt by *you*.

Another example of an add-on that turns a sincere apology into manipulation is asking for help to change your ways: "I am sorry, I missed the payment again. I know it's my responsibility but you know how forgetful I am. Can't you just send me a reminder a couple days before it's due? That way we won't have this argument every month." This particular add-on often leaves people frustrated, disappointed, confused or furious! That's because, even if sincere, it quickly shifts the focus from the other person's pain to your needs, inducing uncomfortable emotions in the very person who ought to be receiving 100% of the focused care and attention.

Statements In Disguise

Statements in disguise are questions that we have already asked and answered internally, and simply want the other person to acknowledge and agree with. For example, "Do you think that was a good decision?" A question like this becomes a manipulative tactic when you don't really want to hear what the person is thinking. The hidden message is that the person in question made the wrong decision and has a poor sense of judgment. These questions are designed to trap the other person, to force them to agree with you and to admit they were wrong.

To put it plainly, when statements in disguise are used, you are not in an open frame of mind. If you're not in an open frame of mind, it will be hard to entertain responses that differ from the answers in your head. In addition, these questions, when asked with our pre-suppositions may sound abrasive, condescending, judgmental and accusatory.

Suggestive Statements

Statements in disguise are not the only types of communication that bare an accusatory tone, suggestive statements do too. Suggestive statements often begin with "I feel like" and end with an accusation. While they are not necessarily manipulative, I mention them here because people often use suggestive statements when they feel manipulated. "I feel like you're trying to take advantage of me" or "I feel like you're only saying sorry to get what you want" are two examples.

Even if someone were to receive a questionable apology, I would suggest avoiding "I feel like" statements for many reasons, but primarily because they are inaccurate and misleading. These statements seem to make a clear connection between our feelings and the facts, but they don't. Even though these statements use the word feel, emotions are not actually labeled. They also skip over the fact that our emotions are usually based on our perceptions about the situations we find ourselves in. In other words, we often feel the way we do based on our thoughts about the situation. Our feelings are just as subjective as our thoughts which can be very inaccurate.

The reality is, our thoughts are not facts. We have thoughts about facts, but that does not make our perspectives, opinions or beliefs factual. Just because we think and subsequently feel something, doesn't make us right. When we express our perspectives as if they are facts, all sorts of other challenges that disrupt healthy communication arise. Take this statement for example, "I feel like you were trying to embarrass me." It speaks to one's conclusion about the other person's intentions, leaving no room for other possibilities, versus, "I feel angry because it seems as if you were trying to embarrass me." An even better option is suspending the anger (based on an unverified conclusion) and simply asking, "Were you trying to embarrass me?"

As opposed to the clarity gained from asking a question, "suggestive" or "I feel like statements" generally result in more tension and conflict.

"Ok Andrew, I can see both the subtle and covert forms manipulation can take but how do I deal with it when it rears its head?"

What To Do If You Think You Are Being Manipulated With An Apology

As the recipient of an apology, it is understandable that you may be skeptical about its sincerity simply because the offence took place. And, if the offence has happened more than once, it's only logical to be unsure about the intentions of the person offering the apology. But, should you have the sense that you are being manipulated, instead of jumping to conclusions or writing the person off, I urge you to seek clarity about their intentions and sincerity to determine if your suspicions are founded. I believe the following illustration will help to put the forms of manipulation into perspective and get a good handle on the strategies to gain the much-needed clarity about the other person's intentions and sincerity.

Shopping Around

Imagine you made the error of lending a friend money *(yes, I said error)*, time passes with no communication from this friend and, one day out of the blue, you literally run into them... at the mall, multiple shopping bags in hand, evidence of a mini shopping spree. Your eyes meet. You are on a collision path. There is nowhere for your friend to run and hide!

As you reach each other they joyously greet you, and say something like, "Oh my goodness, it is sooo good to see you!" After a few moments of rapid fire niceties, they profess that the bags and items are not for them - *Sure!* But before you can get a word out, they look at you as if they've been challenged and offended by something you've said and respond with, "You can look through the bags if you don't believe me." *Awkward!* Then they move on, profusely apologizing for being unable to pay you back, just loud enough for everyone within a 10 metre radius to hear - *Super awkward!!*

Because you're in a public place and want to quickly get through the moment, you try to hide your embarrassment and say as little as possible only to hear them say, "You don't believe me?! I know what you're gonna say, I shouldn't have avoided your calls, but, at first I was really truly very busy and then, well, I was so embarrassed about being unable to pay you back like I promised. If I knew it was gonna put this kind of strain on our friendship, I never would have asked, but things are so bad for me right now... I am so sorry. Please don't be angry with me." Now *you* feel guilty and ashamed, like some sort of unforgiving monster.

Sounds ridiculous, doesn't it? Sadly, too many people can relate to being both the victim and perpetuator of this kind of manipulation. So, what can you do about it? Clarify! The best way to clarify whether or not someone is intentionally or unintentionally manipulating you is by asking very specific questions about *their* intentions and *their* understanding of the facts. In the case of our shopping friend, let's consider some questions that could help dispel the confusion about the situation and get clarity around the facts. Let's imagine you had the wherewithal to pull this friend aside to ask some questions. Here are some examples of questions that could possibly be asked in this situation:

- *Did you really expect me to search through your bags, to see if you were telling me the truth? Do you think I would feel comfortable doing that?*

- *Do you think it's fair for you to ask me to do something like that, in a public place?*

- *Did you not think that I might be utterly mortified by something like that?*

- *I am surprised that you seem shocked that I might not believe you, considering you said you would pay me back in a week and have been avoiding me for months. Do you believe that I should still take you at your word?*

- *You chose not to answer my calls because you were feeling embarrassed and you are in a bad place financially, but did you consider how I was feeling and what I might need?*

- *On top of avoiding me and then addressing this in public, you ask me not to be angry. Do you think it's fair for me to feel angry with you? How do you expect me to feel?*

- *As you pointed out, it has been some time since you received the loan. What other options have you considered in order to pay me back?*

Now, if you're anything like me, this illustration got you a little riled up. You probably even read those questions with an increasingly angry, accusatory and judgmental attitude. And why not, this seems like a clear and blatant disregard for your needs, and your friendship. But now, here's a question for you, when you were reading the possible questions above, how many of them did you presume to know the answer to? All of them, perhaps? Aha! That's the kicker, because, instead of questions, they were actually statements in disguise. If you really want to clarify whether or not you are being manipulated, intentionally or unintentionally, it will be important to refrain from prejudging others with your "questions". If you haven't noticed, I think clarity is pretty important!

This chapter has painted a clear picture of how beautifully sincerity and correctly focused intentions come together to make an apology meaning-full. We've also seen how easily and quickly apologies can become manipulative, even when sincerity and "good intentions" are present. If you're unsettled about the degree of sincerity in your apology or are unsure if your intentions are correctly focused, I encourage you to give thought to the questions below. I have also included some ideas on what to do if you think you are being manipulated and how to avoid unintentionally manipulating the people you care about.

For your consideration

Obtaining clarity is essential and asking specific questions of yourself and others is the best way to go about getting it. As outlined in this chapter, instead of offering an insincere apology (or being duped by one), truly examining yourself, asking very direct questions and remaining open-minded when asking questions can help you to stay on the right side of the very thin line between a meaning-full apology and manipulation.

1.   Clarifying Sincerity

The following questions will help you decide whether or not your apology is sincere:

1) Why am I apologizing?

2) Am I responsible for:

   a) the entire situation?

   b) part of the situation, or

   c) not responsible at all

3) Am I responsible in any way for the other person's pain?

4) If I could do things over, would I change any of my actions?

5) Am I apologizing to make myself feel better?

2. Clarifying Your Intentions

If you are unclear about whether your intentions are correctly focused, you can gain clarity by asking some of the following questions:

1) What exactly am I apologizing for?

2) What do I want to get out of the apology?

3) Is my apology aimed at healing their hurt?

4) What are my reasons for withholding my apology?

5) How do I want this apology to impact the other person?

6) If I knew the other person would not accept my apology, would I still offer it?

7) Am I prepared to endure their reaction?

8) Who is this apology really for?

After answering these questions, you will have a true sense of the purpose of your apology and be absolutely clear about your intentions.

3. Ensuring Your Apology Is Free of Manipulation

The fact that we will hurt the people we love can leave us feeling badly about our choices which can also contribute to our apologies turning into manipulative maneuvers. In addition to ensuring sincerity and correctly focused intentions, there are a few more things to keep in mind to help your apologies to be meaning-full and remain manipulation free.

1) **Avoiding Apology Add-Ons**

If you feel terribly, are thinking horrible things about yourself or are genuinely in need of help or support to change, the following suggestions will help you to remain focused on offering a meaning-full apology:

   a) Save those thoughts and requests for a separate conversation, and

   b) Choose a safe person to address these issues with (someone who will keep your communication to themselves and seek to give you wise and constructive feedback).

2) **Avoiding Statements In Disguise**

As I have pointed out, questions help to provide clarity around intentions. However, in all situations, especially ones that are emotionally charged, try to avoid turning those questions into statements in disguise. If you really want to know whether or not you are being manipulated intentionally or unintentionally, it will be important to refrain from prejudging others with your questions. You can alter the accusatory feel of your questions by doing two important things:

a) Moderate your tone and
b) Be sincerely open and curious about their responses.

Asking questions with genuine curiosity and an openness for explanations that you might not have considered will help you really understand whether or not someone is manipulating you intentionally, unintentionally or even at all.

Take a moment and jump back to the in-debt shopper an re-read the questions that start on page 33. Try to read them as questions rather statements in disguise. I am serious, go back and take a look. Review and repeat those questions with a calm disposition, a moderate tone and, above all, a desire to really hear what the other person has to say. After doing so, I would want to know if you felt different emotions and considered different responses to the same questions.

Not only does a calm and moderate tone as well as an open attitude support a true inquiry about another person's beliefs and intentions in relation to specific facts, it helps to avoid making suggestive statements that assassinate the other person's character and hinder you from obtaining clarity.

3) Avoiding Suggestive Statements

The earlier discussion about suggestive statements noted that, "I feel like" statements express our thoughts about situations in an accusatory fashion often leading to more tension and conflict. Unwittingly, these statements decrease both our ability and our opportunity to be open and receive clarity about the other person's intentions.

To effectively avoid using suggestive statements and successfully pursue clarity be sure to clearly describe how you feel (or felt) in light of the facts. Let's use the in-debt shopper, one final time. A statement like, "I felt so embarrassed when you asked me to check your bags in front of all those people at the mall" clearly labels how you felt when a specific event occurred. It does not present a theory about the intentions of the other person which leaves you in the clear as far as assassinating the other person's character and more open to receive their explanation because you have not jumped to any conclusions.

At the risk of being accused of wasting time and paying too much attention to semantics I will put everything on the line to make this point, words matter! And nowhere do they matter more than when we are hurting and are about to address the people we love. When you are able to ask clarifying questions and refrain from exacerbating situations with statements in disguise and suggestive statements you will be able to acquire a true understanding about the facts and the other person's intentions. Only then will you be able to determine if an apology was more than a manipulative tactic which will ultimately help you decide how to proceed.

I want to wrap up with a reminder of the overarching purpose of this chapter. Whether we are hoping to receive one or attempting to offer one, the purpose of a meaning-full apology is to bring intention and sincerity together to make things right and bring about healing in our most significant relationships. While we can use the suggestions above to pursue clarity and healing, we cannot force people into giving us the apologies we desire, but we can teach them by showing them how it's done.

Perhaps, you are currently wading through the hurt and confusion of a situation with a loved one, or perhaps you're remembering a past situation that you could have handled differently. If you've answered the questions above that are designed to help you ensure that your apology will be sincere, correctly focused and manipulation free, then you get to move past GO!

But, if you are now aware that your apology is not sincere, where do you go from here? Well, let's look to the next page and find out.

Putting in the Work

If you have never been in a situation where someone expected you to offer an apology that you knew would be insincere, get ready because sooner or later, it will happen. Even in the strongest of relationships there will be times when people will struggle with offering a sincere apology. So, what does one do when faced with this dilemma? There are at least 4 options for you to consider:

1) Work towards making your apology sincere

2) Offer an insincere apology

3) Dismiss their complaint entirely and tell them, "The truth hurts, deal with it... I don't care... I'm just being real" or

4) Offer a compassionate acknowledgment of their feelings.

Since this book is all about bringing healing to your most significant relationships through the offering of a Genuine Apology, you might well have deduced that I do not consider options 2 or 3 viable in this process. So, that leaves us with options 1 and 4. We will dive into option 4 in the next chapter, but let's take a look at option 1 and deal with the reality of wanting to be sincere when you are challenged.

Apologizing sincerely can be hard work. If you want to be sincere but are having a hard time, there is a possibility that barriers in the form of thoughts and emotions are blocking sincerity's flow. Thoughts like *I am not wrong*, emotions such as guilt, confusion and anger or issues such as disagreement and conflict, often impede sincerity and the offering of a meaning-full apology. It is here that the hard work of self-examination, a dissection of your own motivations and behaviors, becomes the most critical.

SELF-EXAMINATION

The process of self-examination allows you to thoroughly sort through the issues as you see them and truly look at your own flaws and errors. Very rarely is acknowledging one's errors and flaws a pleasant experience, however, it will help you to arrive at a place of honesty where you can deal with any circumstance free of pretense, self-deceit, and reservations. It can also help to shed light on the emotions that you're feeling when finding it difficult to offer a meaning-full apology.

I can almost see you shaking your head, saying, *"Drew, this whole self-examination thing is not necessary. And besides, I bought this book to figure out how to get (insert whoever's name here) to apologize to me!"* But I guarantee you, enduring this process is pivotal to your success.

Self-examination helps us to sort out how we are feeling, tease these feelings apart from the issues at hand and decide if our initial reactions are valid and appropriate. This is often a complicated but worthwhile venture because our emotions inform all of our interactions. If you agree with me, you will also concede that it makes perfect sense to become adept at recognizing our emotions and being able to respond to situations instead of reacting to them. I call this being "response-able".

Being response-able is actually a skill that helps us to respond in the face of conflict instead of reacting. Being response-able helps us to be responsible. While there is a difference, they work hand in hand. The coordination of the two is particularly valuable when we want to offer a meaning-full apology but are having trouble with sincerity. The only way to do both well is by understanding and managing our emotions. But, emotions are a tricky thing, and none more so than guilt.

Getting A Grip On Guilt

One would think that the feeling of guilt automatically moves people to apologize sincerely, but I have found guilt to be the most confusing emotional barrier to address. Guilt is uniquely challenging for two reasons. First, its tendency to be in flux based on disagreements regarding the facts, questions about the other person's intent and one's own underlying motivations. Second, and even more challenging, it's dual nature. Guilt's duality is derived from being experienced as an emotion as well as a state. This aspect of guilt allows it to be present in varying forms in a single point in time. For example, one can be guilty and feel guilty. However, one can also be guilty and NOT feel guilty at all.

What?? Drew, you have confused me here with this be guilty, feel guilty, not guilty, in flux thing!

Ok, ok. I completely understand. I did mention that it can be the most confusing of the emotional barriers to address, so let me break it down further using this next scenario.

📖 Changes In One Brother's Emotional Apology

Act I - Driving me crazy

Wanting to ensure he is on time for a very important work meeting that could change everything for him, a brother borrows his sister's brand new car. On his way to the office, another driver starts to merge into his lane. Realizing he is in the other car's blind spot, he immediately begins to honk his horn but they just keep coming!! Thinking he can swerve to avoid being hit, he frantically looks around but, there is nowhere for him to go. In the blink of an eye it's over. He's been hit! In that moment, all he can say to himself over and over again, is, "I just wrecked my sister's brand new car!"

After the ordeal of statements to the Police, calling the insurance company and cancelling his work meeting, he makes his way home with a heavy heart. He knows his sister will be terribly upset considering how much trust she placed in him, letting him use her brand-new car.

Passenger-side front panel dented, bumper badly scratched, the pit of his stomach tightly wrenched with emotions, he arrives home. Even while bracing himself for what is to come, there is a sliver of hope that despite how angry she'll be, she'll understand. After all, everyone involved, including the Police, agreed that the accident was not his fault. Truly sorry for what has happened and feeling certain that he could not have done any more to avoid the outcome, he breaks the news to his sister. "Helena, I was in an accident on my way to work, I am soooo sorry." She is upset, as he knew she would be. But what he doesn't expect are the accusations and cutting character assassination. She calls him reckless and goes as far as stating his carelessness is really about him being jealous because she is the favored child! Shocked and unable to respond, he stands silent, enduring the onslaught. But, as the shock wears off, hurt and anger begin to set in and he wonders, "How could she possibly think this way about me?!"

Let's pause and tease this scenario apart. I want to identify the facts as well as the emotions and explore how quickly anger joins the confusing fray resulting in a more contentious dynamic that moves this brother further away from guilt and a meaning-full apology.

FACT, he is guilty of driving his sister's car and being involved in an accident. And even though, from his perspective, the accident was purely that, an accident, if he had not borrowed her brand-new car it would not have been damaged and for this, he *feels* guilty. Filled with remorse he immediately offers her a meaning-full apology. Not only is it sincere, but it is correctly focused. His apology does not attempt to secure his innocence, rather it is totally focused on her loss.

However, there is more at play here. Let's focus on two things that are changing in rapid succession as the story unfolds: the brother's emotions and his apology.

Act II - Oh what a tangled web!

With each accusation and attack on his character, this brother's feelings of guilt drift further and further away and the remaining emotions become entangled and inflamed. Within seconds he has moved from feeling remorse and guilt to shock and hurt. To his credit these unpleasant emotions are graciously accepted and quickly soothed by empathy because he can imagine being just as angry if the shoe was on the other foot. However, this moment of understanding succumbs to confusion as his sister's outlandish interpretation of childhood squabbles long-forgotten continues and again somehow culminates in his intentionally wrecking her car. Now, he is seething with anger.

As he repeatedly utters the words, "I'm sorry… I'm sorry… I'm sorry…", he's thinking to himself, *"How could she say something like that? Nobody talks to me this way!! Who does she think she is?! She hasn't even asked me if I am ok?!!"*

To quell his own fury and keep himself from losing it, he attempts to muster up some more empathy for her reaction. Yet, with every additional "I'm sorry" he struggles more and more with enduring and excusing her over-the-top behavior. His meaning-full apology disintegrates into meaningless words offered to appease his sister's feelings and shield himself from her anger as well as his own. For, while he's ok with accepting blame for the accident, he is waking to the fact that he is silently accepting a host of unsavory descriptions of his character.

As both the shock of the accident and his tolerance for her rant completely wears away, he comes to himself and realizes that his repeated apologies have shifted from being sincere to desperate attempts to get her to just stop talking. In fact, this brother's apology has been drained of all sincerity. At this point, offering a meaning-full apology is not even a consideration as feelings of guilt and remorse have been violently washed away by her reaction and replaced with his intense anger. Now he wishes he had not apologized at all.

Towards the end of chapter 2 we highlighted one of the dangers of an insincere apology, allowing others to remain unaware of their problematic behavior and escape ownership of their actions. This situation is a prime example of how an apology can be a very unhelpful thing. Enduring an offensive and hurtful rant while saying, "I'm sorry" can allow someone to think their behavior is acceptable. With his focus on soothing the intense conflict and hers on expressing intense anger, both fail to make a distinction between the facts surrounding the accident and their emotional reactions to the accident.

Although this brother's apology is sincere at the onset, as his sister's belligerent behavior continues and his feelings change, his apology also changes. It is no longer meaning-full and is unable to bring about healing in this situation. In theory, the opposite now becomes more likely. Can you foresee the resentment and eventual estrangement that could grow between this brother and sister if the hurtful and offensive rant is left unaddressed?

While not all situations involve so much fluctuation, it is a necessary discussion. If not properly handled, conflict has a tendency to balloon into hurtful exchanges where feelings of regret, guilt and remorse are eclipsed by anger. Experiences like this can lead to perpetual internal conflict and indecision on just how to move forward. Some families have been caught in this kind of conflict for years, to the point that no one even remembers why they are not speaking to each other.

While the details of this brother and sister's conflict may differ from stories you've heard or experienced, the reality of being swept away by our emotions when in conflict with the people closest to us is more common than we'd like to admit. Again, being response-able is a skill to be honed by everyone who chooses to love other imperfect people. Should you find yourself moving further and further away from sincerity and meaning-full apologies, carried away by anger and resentment as a result of hurtful conflict, I believe the following strategies can be of help.

For your consideration

To prevent anger from robbing you of sincerity and high jacking your emotions as well as your apologies give thought to these two strategies:

1. Take A Breather

Instead of reacting defensively, literally take a moment away from the situation. The sooner you stop the progression of this kind of interaction the easier it will be to pull yourself out and regroup.

2. Secure Sincerity

Return to the questions asked in the previous chapter to reconnect with your initial desire to sincerely address the other person's pain.

Although these two steps sound easy, they will take practice, time and herculean effort. If you've successfully taken these two steps and have done the hard work of self-examination and truly believe you are not responsible for any aspect the other person's pain then, NOT apologizing may be the most appropriate course of action.

Wait, what?! Now I'm really confused Drew. Ahhh, yes, I thought you might be. Not to worry, this is where we move to option 4.

Chapter Four

To Apologize or Not to Apologize...that is the question!

Now, why would I encourage not apologizing in a book about cultivating the art of a Genuine Apology? The answer is simple, to ensure sincerity. Saying sorry before really taking the time to sort through the feelings and issues connected to the situation can often leave individuals feeling upset and filled with regret. These emotions make perfect sense because when we apologize insincerely, we are being dishonest with ourselves as well as with others.

And, just in case it has not been made abundantly clear, this also applies to apologizing for things we are not responsible for. Accepting blame and unduly taking responsibility denies us, and everyone else involved, the opportunity to address the real issues. This course of action sets us up to experience incessant regret and resentment, something I like to call "apologizer's remorse".

This book is not just about learning how to apologize well, it's also an encouragement to give adequate thought to your apologies so you can avoid apologizer's remorse. When we only offer apologies when it is appropriate to do so, we are saving ourselves from wishing we could take our apologies back.

Please don't get me wrong, I am not saying never apologize if you feel conflicted. Nor am I suggesting that you passionately declare that you are not sorry for doing or saying something hurtful as if speaking "your truth" is the whole point of the conversation (which some people actually believe). While authenticity is one of the most important things in the world to me, compassion is also something I would never want you, or I, to live without. What I am saying is, there is a balance. Healthy relationships need authenticity and compassion. You can tell the truth with love and be honest with compassion. So then, how are we to handle a situation where an apology may be expected but is not appropriate? I happily present to you, the Compassionate Acknowledgment.

THE COMPASSIONATE ACKNOWLEDGEMENT

After you've done the hard work of self-examination

and still believe you are not responsible for any aspect the other person's pain a compassionate acknowledgement will help you land in a place where regret and resentment are unable to find you. What, exactly, is a compassionate acknowledgment? It is a sincere expression that positions you right where love and truth intersect. A clear and cohesive statement that acknowledges the facts of the situation, shows compassion for the other person's feelings as well as shares your perspective without apologizing. Bringing these elements together, honestly and respectfully, can be very difficult, especially when experiencing intense emotions. Very few people have been taught just how to do this.

Even after many years of helping others to address challenging situations, I still find it challenging to strike this balance when I am upset or hurt. Finding this balance is hard! Quite often, in our attempts to find this place in the middle we oscillate from one end of the spectrum to the other; carelessly vomiting our "truth" on each other or burying the actual truth and silencing our feelings. And back and forth we go. Both extremes, whether unleashing our fury or suppressing our thoughts and emotions can lead to internal conflict, confusion and indecision about how to move forward in a healthy, fruitful and authentic way. It is my desire to break this cycle and help people bring an end to their hurtful patterns. The road to strengthening our most significant relationships will bring us to these conversations time and time again. I want us all to be prepared to honestly acknowledge challenging situations with compassion.

I am not an unrealistic optimist. I accept that conflict is inevitable, but I am also aware that mature and loving responses optimize the growth within every conflict. Respectfully addressing facts and feelings that trouble us and authentically expressing our perspectives while tending to the emotions of others with love is the goal of a compassionate acknowledgment. Yes, it's a tall order, but it is possible! To help us gain a clear understanding of a compassionate acknowledgment, let's take a look at a mother and father team at odds over balancing the budget and meeting the "needs" of their only son.

 The Buck Stops Here

Act I - Here we go again

After repeated discussions about budgeting and saving, Jenny cringes as her husband walks in the door with a Razor Hovertrax for their son. For those of you who don't know, this wonderfully exciting futuristic version of a skateboard has a value of over $500. With audible disappointment Jenny says, "Tony, I know that you want James to have everything in the world, especially the things you didn't have as a kid, but we discussed this. It's putting a strain on our budget and I am tired of living this way! We just can't afford any additional expenses right now. We really need to stick to our budget and manage our finances responsibly!"

Despite having had this conversation many times before, Tony is upset and believes that Jenny is really talking about him and his spending habits. His shame and guilt are quickly concealed by anger and he responds, "So, you think I'm irresponsible... no good with money and can't do anything right, hunh? Well, I'm not the only one who spends money on things we don't need! And besides, don't you want our son to have the best things life has to offer? Why are you always pointing out my flaws? Don't I do anything right?!?"

Of course, Tony does some things right. That is not at all what Jenny is trying to say. She has no intention to hurt or offend him. Despite this instance of budgetary weakness, Jenny knows how hard he tries not to spend beyond their limits and how horrible he feels when these fights happen. Jenny is moved with sympathy and her first instinct is to offer a heartfelt apology.

But my question to you is, what is she really sorry about? Is she truly sorry that she shared her feelings and thoughts or is her regret that her partner was offended and hurt by what she said? These types of situations are precisely what this chapter aims to explore and address.

Being genuinely impacted by the hurt or offended emotional responses of the people we care about is a healthy reaction. Unfortunately, for the majority of people, it triggers an immediate apology. Even though we may be sincerely sympathetic or sincerely empathize with how terrible someone is feeling, the presence of these emotions does not automatically qualify a situation for an apology. In cases like these, when offered only to soothe an offence taken, an apology would be misguided and most likely understood as a retraction of one's truest thoughts. In these situations, a compassionate acknowledgement would be the most appropriate response. Fortunately for us, this is the type of situation Jenny is in, once again. Let's see how she responds to Tony.

Act II - The Compassionate Acknowledgement in Action

"Tony, I can see that you're upset by what I am saying to you and it makes me feel really sad. You're a wonderful father and you do many great things for our family. I honestly appreciate everything you do for us. I hope you can understand that I just want things to be better for us financially and for you to make different choices when it comes to the budget."

Instead of trying to force sincerity into an insincere apology or apologizing when she is not responsible for Tony's hurt, Jenny compassionately acknowledges the impact her statements have had on Tony. You can see that Jenny avoided saying "I'm sorry" or using an unhelpful phrase like "I am sorry that you feel that way, but..."

While it can be especially challenging to avoid using the word "but" or taking responsibility when you offer a compassionate acknowledgment, it is extremely important. The aim, here, is to sincerely express empathy without compromising authenticity. Like I said before, healthy relationships need authenticity as well as compassion. A compassionate acknowledgement of another person's feelings can strike the delicate balance between authenticity and compassion every time!

As you can imagine, it takes a considerable amount of skill to instantly respond to the hurt reactions of the people we care about with truth and compassion. Although this is a skill that can be honed over time with lots of practice, I dare to say, "instantly" responding with a compassionate acknowledgment is not possible until it becomes a part of who we are. Having it move beyond being an effective strategy and becoming a disposition that permeates all of our interactions is my ultimate goal.

So, how does one do this? How can you get there?

I have two worthwhile strategies for you to ponder.

For your consideration

1. Taking The Time

I am personally aware that getting to the point of effectively, skillfully and naturally extending a compassionate acknowledgment takes time. Time is obviously a key factor in cultivating this approach, but "taking time" is also a strategy in and of itself. Whether we are offering a compassionate acknowledgement or an apology, sometimes we need to take time before responding. Taking time can help to gather our thoughts and be clear and intentional about what we want to say. Now that you've read about a compassionate acknowledgment, taking the time would be the first step towards offering it.

I admit, when people first hear the idea of taking time or someone asking for time in the middle of an intense conversation to consider whether or not they want to apologize, they find it ludicrous. But honestly letting the person know you want time to respond can be very helpful.

Momentarily leaving conversations on a civil note helps us to sincerely consider; consider what we could have done differently, how to move forward and whether or not the situation requires an apology or a compassionate acknowledgment. Sometimes that takes a couple of minutes and other times a couple of hours or even days. So, while it may be uncomfortable for the other person to excuse you, take a break from the conversation and allow you to return to it at another time, this is often beneficial for both parties.

Navigating these situations can be tough, especially when you sense that an apology is expected. Nevertheless, this strategy is not aimed at avoiding conflict. It's target, once again, is sincerity. It is important to keep the goal of sincerity at the forefront of our minds and to realize that each of our conversations are laying the groundwork for future interactions.

Hmmm...I hadn't thought of it that way, Drew. I really like this idea of "taking time" but, how do I bring that up in a conversation, or worse, an argument?

Have you ever heard the phrase, "It's not what you say but how you say it?" Honestly letting the person know you want time to respond can be very helpful, but won't stand a chance if you use a statement like this, "I am not sure if you deserve an apology. Let me think about it and get back to you!" Even though you may have good intentions, this kind of statement does not convey a compassionate acknowledgement of the other person's hurt, it does not prioritize or address the needs of the person you are speaking to first and, quite frankly, it sounds as if you're assessing whether or not the person is even worth an apology!

Can you imagine how it would feel to be on the receiving end of that kind of statement? Instead, something like this will likely embody the tone you wish to convey and be more effective, "You know, it seems like you are really upset about the whole situation and I am too. I need a moment to gather my thoughts so that I can really listen and process everything so this conversation can be productive." Here is another example, "I can see you're upset by what I've said and I'm feeling defensive. Let me take some time to calm down before we continue this conversation."

In direct contrast to the off-putting statement noted earlier, both of these examples clearly identify your need for time but also acknowledge the other person's feelings. These statements inherently accomplish three things: 1) communicate your awareness of the other person's emotions, 2) express a commitment to return to the conversation which achieves the last objective 3) convey a message of significant value for the relationship. These three endeavours will help the other person to be more open to your request for time.

2. Defining The Amount Of Time

The idea of taking time offers an intentional and strategic approach to sharing a meaning-full apology or a compassionate acknowledgment with healing and love as the finish line of each experience. If you want to use this strategy and make it to this finish line alive, being specific about the amount of time you intend to take is absolutely essential. All jokes aside, if you're not specific about how much time you will take before returning to the issue, the other person may grow impatient and come back to you before you've had enough time to figure out how you want to respond. Specifying the amount of time needed helps the other person to be patient and helps you remain committed to returning to the conversation.

Be mindful as you make requests to take time, that if promises to revisit issues have been made and not kept, whether by you or someone else, this person may not trust that there will be a return to the conversation and may even view this as a manipulative tactic. Even though you may not have intentionally manipulated the person in the past, they may be leery and have their guard up. This is why it will always be of benefit to be specific about how much time you need. Over time, if you're consistent, you will have a better chance of regaining the other person's trust.

With that said, defining the amount of time you need can be hard to assess in the moment. So, how should this be handled? I believe it's best to overestimate and take more time than you think you might actually need. By giving yourself at minimum a few hours to a day to consider the issue, you'll likely be able to think things through and decide how you want to proceed. If the time you've requested elapses and you are no closer to formulating a response, be sure to connect with the person and let them know that you would like to take more time.

You might be thinking, *Taking a whole day is not necessary and no one would go for that!* The reality is most arguments are followed by a silent aftermath of stomach-churning tension or passive aggressive behavior that lasts much longer than a day. Trust me, taking the time will save you time and emotional energy. It might just save your relationship!

While the strategies discussed in this chapter might save your relationship, it cannot save you from conflict. So, please don't fall prey to the temptation to use it for that purpose. Whether you are compassionately acknowledging someone's feelings or taking time to avoid offering an insincere apology, using these approaches to deceive or outsmart someone even for the sake of avoiding conflict moves past being strategic to being manipulative. Like I said before, conflict is inevitable, but a mature and loving response can change the course of your conversations and your relationship.

At this point we've discussed many things that will at the very least provide a substantial platform for you to open dialogue with the people you care the most about. But, if you desire to really bring healing to your most significant relationships, you will need to ascend to the highest level of apologies and cultivate the "art" of a Genuine Apology. And, it is to that level of apologies we now turn.

CHAPTER FIVE

The "Genuine Apology"

In chapter one we defined a basic apology as an expression that acknowledges one's actions that have impacted another with regret. Chapter two moved on to discuss the need for a deeper level of apology, the meaning-full apology, where good intentions and sincerity focus on seeking the best interest of the hurt or offended party first. Now we will venture into the deepest most complex level of apologies.

The circumstances that require the kind of apology that I want to address in the remaining chapters of this book are often very broad, ranging from seemingly trivial moments that somehow manage to induce inexplicable reactions to obviously hurtful situations that are so injurious that you'd like to erase them from your memory. In the wake of these experiences with the people we love the most we need more than what the apologies discussed so far provide. We will journey far beyond past experiences of inadequate apologies into a world of authentic interactions that create environments ripe with healing. Even though we will still experience moments of confusion, tension, anger, embarrassment, shame and gut wrenching guilt, in this informed and purposeful place of healing, as opposed to being instruments of pain, the expressions of our truest sentiments become the balm for invisible wounds. As fantastical as it may seem, we can grasp and skillfully wield the whys, the whats, and the hows that facilitate the healing of this deepest level of apology.

Singer Dan Hill asks, "Why do we always hurt the ones we love?" While I don't believe we always, that is consistently or repetitively, hurt the ones we love, I agree that hurting them and being hurt by them is inevitable. For me, what makes this reality painfully saddening is that unaddressed hurts eventually cause love and compassion to dissipate leaving most people unprepared, and some even unwilling, to extend or receive the kind of apology that breathes new life into their relationships. Relationships deprived of the care, understanding and healthy communication embodied by this level of apology inescapably become the burial grounds of tenderness and compassion.

Why should I open myself to hearing their perspective or addressing their pain when I am hurting too? How can I show care and compassion to the person who hurt me? Do I have to do this? These are the questions that guard our hearts and are often answered in ways that keep us from taking the necessary steps inherent to the process of healing. I know it is daunting to think that the healing of our deepest hurts asks us to be vulnerable and loving with the very people who have, and still can, wound us. Nevertheless, whether we are offering or waiting to receive an apology, if we are unable to wrap our minds around this endeavour and be willing to follow this course of action, then we'll be stuck nursing wounds that will never truly be healed. Moving beyond hurt and deep emotional injury demands the readiness and capacity to offer, and receive, this deepest level of apology.

Unlike some "let's-get-it-over-with-drive-by apologies", where a rapid fire one-size fits all apology gets haphazardly sprayed hoping to hit the right target, this apology is not a simple, pre-loaded, pre-scripted, one-way expression limited to a single shooting, I mean, conversation. It requires so much more than a trite concession or an offering of guilt-ridden resignation, "You're right. I'm wrong. I'm sorry". It is the kind of apology that calls for heartfelt investment (uninhibited, passionate determination and sacrifice) as well as critical thinking (analysis, evaluation and planning). Only those who are committed to every aspect of this apology will be able to see it through to its end.

While the demands are high, this level of apology is worth it! It effectively addresses the deepest of wounds and holds the power to free both the giver and the receiver from prisons of loneliness. The key to unlock the shackles of anger, bitterness, resentment and guilt is a "Genuine Apology".

While I would love to proceed with a succinct definition of a Genuine Apology, one just does not exist. You see, there is no simple, easily memorized definition because the offering of a Genuine Apology moves beyond reciting prescribed words or a simplistic set of steps. However, as we need some basis from which to begin our journey into this new interactive level of the ultimate apology, I will provide you the following as a guide: An apology that brings good intentions, sincerity, thoughtfulness, effective delivery and healing together. An apology that intentionally shows the kind of care and understanding that validates the giver and the receiver. An apology that requires and demonstrates the type of listening and expression that gives hope for rebuilding and reinstating value in relationships. This is how I would endeavour to define a Genuine Apology and it is what this book is all about.

Herein Lies The Art

As our title proclaims, there is an art to offering a Genuine Apology. As in life, mastery of any discipline requires a thorough understanding of foundational principles as well as consistent practical application through guided and repetitious practice. Our discussion to this point has sought to lay a good foundation upon which we will build our understanding of the Genuine Apology. With respect to the guidance needed, I would love to hear from you directly and offer any support I can. But until then, I will remain confident that the remainder of this book will offer valuable direction on how to incorporate the essential aspects of offering a Genuine Apology as you move towards healing your most significant relationships.

The pages and chapters ahead offer an in depth understanding of the components that create a Genuine Apology, the indicators and results of a Genuine Apology as well as the steps to building one with your words and your actions. Yes, your words and your actions. Although this is a book that serves as a guide, this is also an interactive process that engages with real life. As you will come to see, not only will a Genuine Apology inform all of your most heartfelt conversations but it will also guide your actions, creating a framework for future challenging yet loving interactions. Most importantly, a Genuine Apology will live on long after it has been shared.

THE WORKING PARTS OF A GENUINE APOLOGY

Offering a Genuine Apology incorporates two very significant parts; the first is all about the essential substance and composition of the apology and the second, is all about the packaging and delivery. Building on the meaning-full apology, that requires sincerity and correctly focused intentions, the necessary ingredients for a Genuine Apology also include these 5 key values: Humility, Vulnerability, Empathy, Responsibility and Accountability. The second part of the apology, the packaging and delivery, will be shared in 4 steps and is best remembered by the acronym L.I.V.E.:

1) List and label the specific behaviors for which you are apologizing = L

2) Imagine and express the impact you believe your actions have had = I

3) Verbalize your commitment to change and a plan of action = V

4) Extend an invitation for the person to respond to your apology = E

As in dancing, there is a world of authentic passion-filled mastery beyond learning the steps. So too with perfecting the art of a Genuine Apology. In learning and practicing these steps you will, initially, feel clumsy and awkward. However, in time, your cautious and sometimes labored execution, will give way to a natural, graceful expression as you embody a new way of addressing hurt and L.I.V.E. out your Genuine Apology. This becomes the art.

And so, as we venture further together, I am encouraging thoughtful consideration of these values with the hope of deepening your understanding and appreciation of what a Genuine Apology is and why it is not only beneficial but required in order to move from a place of stagnation and pain into growth and healing.

As we move into this most involved experience of apologies, we will, of course examine the role of the key values and the steps that define and make up this way of attending to our hurts and those of the people we love the most. But first, I want to acknowledge those of you who may be thinking that this is a lot of work. As with anything new, you may be feeling nervous and unsure but I don't want you to talk yourself out of moving ahead. Perhaps, the following questions will remind you of moments that will make moving forward worth it. At the very least, they will prepare you for where we are about to go.

For your consideration

1. Have you received an apology that may have been sincere but still didn't quite hit the spot? What would you say was missing from that apology?
2. Have you offered a sincere apology yet are perplexed as to why the person is having a hard time accepting your apology and letting the issue go?
3. Have you asked the person what is making it hard for them to accept your apology? If not, what stops you from asking?

CHAPTER SIX

The 5 Essential Values of a Genuine Apology

No matter who we are or at what stage of life we find ourselves, relationships matter. Whether we observe the love between parent and child, husband and wife, sisters and brothers or the bond between friends, we see that these relationships shape us, ground us and remain some of the most influential, rewarding and vital experiences we will ever have. They can also house some of the most stressful, combative and devastating experiences too.

As a result, unaddressed issues that seed intense and unpleasant emotions like anger, bitterness, resentment and guilt, fertilized by our own negative thoughts, can grow into forest like emotional difficulties, contributing to anxiety and depression, and unhealthy choices such as substance use and infidelity. Not only can unresolved issues and unaddressed hurts contribute to all sorts of emotional issues, they affect the physical domain of our lives as well.

Stress, anger, rage, resentment and bitterness have long been credited as contributing factors to physical ailments ranging from fatigue to the exacerbation of diseases as devastating as cancer. If these kinds of emotions can bring about such pain and havoc in our lives, then logically, addressing the issues that lead to them can contribute to healing the emotional, psychological and physical conditions we experience as well.

While the reasons for not directly addressing the hurts we've endured or caused may seem limitless and even understandable, a willingness to consider a new way forward, particularly through giving and receiving Genuine Apologies, can be the doorway to freedom and healing. I imagine that many people may be afraid to take the next step, to approach the doorway and cross the threshold of the Genuine Apology. When faced with admitting your culpability for the harm caused to the most important people in your life it's easy to imagine things going horribly wrong and the worst of your fears coming to life. In moments like these, it is easy to wonder, *Can an apology fix this? Is this relationship ruined beyond repair? What will they say? Will they listen to anything I have to say?* These questions run through our minds, toy with our emotions, hold us hostage and cause many of us to shrink away from attempting to apologize.

Although I can't answer these questions for you, I can say with great confidence, the best way to find the answers to these questions is to brave the untraveled road of your Genuine Apology. In order to confidently head down this road, prepared for whatever lies ahead, you will need to move beyond regret and into remorse. Understanding and embracing the values embedded within a Genuine Apology will help you to do just that. So, let's examine these values to ensure we understand what remorse really is, starting with humility.

HUMILITY

From start to finish, humility is woven throughout a Genuine Apology. Some people cringe at the word humility, because it sounds like (and might have been) associated with humiliation. But humility and humiliation are two very different things. Humility is actually a good thing. Humility does not leave us cowering to the wishes and abuse of others or believing that one is worth less than another. Unlike humiliation, that intentionally seeks to erode a person's self-worth, humility simply acknowledges that we are all human, imperfect and subject to error. Imperfection is part of the human condition. Does this mean we are forever destined for perpetual mistakes and actions that undermine our most significant relationships? No! I choose to believe it means the exact opposite. Our imperfections highlight opportunities to grow as individuals and have better relationships. Humility enables us to acknowledge and seize these opportunities.

Again, humility is a good thing and can have a positive impact on every facet of our lives. Contrary to the attitude of "always being right", a humble disposition relinquishes claims to such titles and is invested in learning and changing for the better. The impact that humility can have in our relationships is monumental! It is the starting point of a shared experience of growth and reliance on each other for mutual, open and honest feedback which leads to change. Humility helps us to be open to change and allows us to take the first step towards offering a Genuine Apology.

As humans, we are going to make mistakes, unwise decisions and fall short of expectations (ours and those of the people we care about). Intentionally or unintentionally, as I mentioned earlier, we will hurt the ones we love at some point in time. Whether you are focused on the hurt that you've caused or the hurt that you've endured, the fact that no one gets everything right all of the time is a humbling reality, a reality that is important to accept. The good news is, that we can do our best to address those hurts by offering Genuine Apologies.

I have found that, without fail, humility significantly decreases conflict and increases the effectiveness of one's apology. Humility can also impact the receptiveness of the person you are apologizing to in a very profound way. When people experience an apology bathed in humility, hostility and anger tend to give way to understanding and warmth. Yet and still, be aware that walking in and practicing humility involves significant risk. There is no shaking the fact that true humility naturally lends to vulnerability, an experience most of us are, in some way, afraid of.

VULNERABITLITY

Humbly offering an apology that acknowledges our mistakes and unwise choices leaves us vulnerable, open to criticism, rejection, shame and possible attack. Not only is an admission of failure enough to warrant criticism from others, but we are often our own worst critics, berating ourselves long after conversations with others have ended. Some people refuse to apologize for this very reason, having to deal with themselves. Admitting that you've done something wrong and hurtful to someone you love can be devastating, striking a terrible blow to your sense of self and identity. Nevertheless, I have come to believe that vulnerability is absolutely necessary in order to offer a Genuine Apology. The choice to be vulnerable purposefully moves us beyond acknowledging the fact that everyone makes mistakes to a recognition of our personal errors and faults.

Hmmm...ok Andrew, who really wants to make themselves vulnerable to embarrassment, ridicule and rejection? Is apologizing worth all of that? I believe it is! Whether we are thinking about spouses, family members or friends, we cherish these relationships because we believe we are known and accepted in them. This is what it means to belong.

So, when we've done wrong and believe this acceptance and belonging is threatened by the possibility of others seeing us differently and distancing themselves from us, we feel vulnerable and may be tempted to retreat into denial of our wrongs, hide behind defensive responses or offer coerced superficial apologies in order to avoid feelings of embarrassment, disappointment and rejection. But I believe vulnerability is intrinsically connected to acceptance. People can only accept or reject what we actually reveal. Vulnerability not only makes you accessible to the other person, it is the very thing that allows the other person to really know you. Without being vulnerable and sharing ourselves completely, we can't truly be known or accepted.

A Genuine Apology is a bold gesture that enables us to come out of hiding and be vulnerable. While this may sound like something to run away from, part of entering into a world of authentic interactions and effectively creating a safe environment for healing involves demonstrating that you not only have vulnerabilities but are willing to share them.

Vulnerability And The Committed Relationship

Opportunities to be vulnerable occur daily in committed relationships. I have come to realize that vulnerability leads to deeper intimacy and deeper intimacy leads to greater vulnerability. If you want a deeper relationship, continually making the most of these opportunities is the best thing to do. It's a never-ending, sometimes terrifying cycle that establishes and deepens relationships. This cycle enables couples to know each other better and better instead of growing apart. You cannot have true intimacy without vulnerability. Refusing to be vulnerable will only lock you into relationships that will never truly be intimate. Many marriages fail or become stagnant because people avoid the act of being vulnerable. Ironically, being vulnerable with people outside of a marriage is often what cultivates the intimacy that leads to infidelity.

EMPATHY

Just like vulnerability, experiencing and employing empathy is knitted intricately throughout a Genuine Apology and is a key factor in strengthening relationships. Experiencing and expressing empathy allows others to know that you understand what they are feeling and how you've affected them. Many people confuse sympathy with empathy because they sound similar, but they are very different. While sympathy is associated with the apologetic words of comfort that we offer in times of bereavement, sympathy has no place in the Genuine Apology. A Genuine Apology is not offered out of pity. It is offered because we have wronged someone. Empathy moves us far past feeling sorry for someone and reaches far beyond simply acknowledging error. It connects the dots between our actions, the other person's experience of our actions and our emotions about their experience.

Is there a way to tell when you're experiencing empathy? Most definitely! When you can relate and even feel similar emotions, if not the very same emotions to some degree as another person, you know you are experiencing empathy. For example, when I hear someone talk about the unpredictable waves of sadness that creep up on them as they grieve the loss of a loved one, I can relate and easily recall similar experiences. Whether I offer condolences or communicate support with a hug or a hand on the shoulder, in these moments I am experiencing and exercising empathy. When we feel sorry for others, we are sympathetic, but when we relate to others, grieve on some level with them and find ways to convey our emotions and support, then we are being empathetic.

Empathy, Regret And Remorse

Just as empathy takes us beyond sympathy when acknowledging loss, when it comes to offering a Genuine Apology empathy moves us past regret and into remorse. Many people feel regret for what they've done, but are not remorseful. If you are not remorseful, you cannot offer a Genuine Apology!

So, what is the difference between regret and remorse? A simplistic explanation would say regret is focused on the cost to one's self while remorse is focused on the pain we've caused someone else. The difference lies in the empathy or lack of empathy experienced for the other person. When people regret their actions because they were caught or there is some sort of consequence, they are not necessarily remorseful and would likely do it again if they weren't going to get caught. But when we experience remorse, there is a degree of sadness and sorrow felt over the pain our actions have caused.

When you experience empathy, truly appreciating the pain you've caused another person, then you are that much closer to demonstrating the capacity needed for this kind of apology. Being humble, vulnerable and empathetic contributes to our readiness and willingness to offer a Genuine Apology. If someone is not ready and fails to demonstrate humility, risk vulnerability and lacks empathy they are not going take responsibility or be receptive to accountability, which are the final two values inherent to a Genuine Apology.

RESPONSIBILITY AND ACCOUNTABILITY

While empathy relies heavily on emotions to connect the heart of the offender to the offended, responsibility and accountability are the values that depend heavily on one's willingness and ability to think objectively and critically. These values help us to revisit the past, tolerate the discomfort of the present and make clear and worthwhile declarations about the future. Chapters 11-14 will share exactly how this is done, but in essence, accepting responsibility and being open to accountability enables the offender to effectively create a safe place for the offended party who gets to carefully assess the degree of safety as they consider the offender's Genuine Apology.

After significant hurt, accepting someone's apology may be quick but should not be automatic. Careful examination of an apology is not only understandable it is important. Many people fail to understand what makes it so hard for people to get over things that have happened in the past, however, if you really think about it, it makes sense to be unwilling and even unable to launch into a future filled with skepticism and fear because the past has not been sufficiently addressed.

Without adequately addressing the past and the future, the way forward will be fraught with fear, mistrust and anger. As such, responsibility and accountability will always be present in a Genuine Apology. If someone is offering a Genuine Apology they will accept responsibility for their actions. There is absolutely no compromise with this! Many people want to shy away from taking responsibility and want to smooth things over with a quick "I'm sorry", but a Genuine Apology will feature both an acknowledgement of wrongdoing and acceptance of responsibility.

What if you want to offer an apology but don't know exactly why the person is so upset? Can you offer a Genuine Apology if you don't know what you are responsible for? That's a great question. I am aware that sometimes, we may be at a loss for what we have done to hurt someone. Thankfully, we can still make our way towards offering a Genuine Apology. If you are prepared to offer a Genuine Apology you will be open to hearing the other person's perspective about what you have done wrong. This kind of openness demonstrates the humility we discussed earlier and paves the way for accepting responsibility. Even if you don't agree entirely with their perspective you will be willing to accept responsibility for something. You may have to take the time to search for an aspect that you believe you are responsible for, but a sincere search often yields an opportunity for changing something that is worthy of acknowledgement and is meaningful to the other person.

The willingness to search for something and to take ownership of some part of the interaction benefits both parties. This willingness makes the difference between being blamed and taking responsibility. Blame usually incites anger and rarely results in long lasting change. When people take responsibility, on the other hand, they are much more open to doing whatever it takes to avoid the situation happening again, which lends to being accountable.

Experiencing accountability can be challenging but one's openness to being accountable is essential to repairing a significant breach in a relationship, which is what Genuine Apologies seek to accomplish. As noted earlier, accountability connects the present moment with the future that one hopes to build. Because the future is unknown, accountability is especially vital to one's Genuine Apology. Accountability is the immediate evidence one can provide that acknowledges their awareness of the possibility for a particular incident to happen again as well as their true desire for it not to happen again.

When embraced by the party offering the apology, accountability helps to retain the responsibility of avoiding future occurrences as opposed to sharing that responsibility or placing it entirely on the hurt party (like the apology add-on of asking someone for help to change). Unfortunately, many people are not aware of how critical accountability is in breaking the cycle of hurt in relationships. If the right arrangement of accountability is not defined the hurt party inevitably becomes the enforcer which leads to several unfortunate outcomes, namely, increased blame, increased shame, decreased vulnerability, decreased intimacy, decreased empathy on both sides and a continuation of the hurtful cycle.

Another thing that many people fail to realize about accountability is that it is the very thing that breathes life into an apology and keeps the apology current. Some people find themselves apologizing for a past offense over and over again. Daily accountability takes the place of repeating an apology and revives the original apology by moving it out of the past, into the present and on into the future.

While each person and each offence will require a different apology, each and every Genuine Apology will embody humility, vulnerability, empathy, responsibility and accountability. It is these 5 values that make a Genuine Apology powerful! Before we take a look at just how powerful a Genuine Apology can be, I have some questions for you to consider.

For your consideration

1. How much value do you place on humility, vulnerability, empathy, responsibility and accountability?

2. Which of these values do you see operating in your most significant relationships on a daily basis?

3. Which of these values do you find most difficult to live out consistently? What contributes to it being such a challenge?

CHAPTER SEVEN

The Bridge between Forgiveness and Reconciliation

Only 48 hours after the murder of her mother in the Charleston Shooting on June 17th of 2015, Nadine Collier, daughter of Ethel Lance, one of 9 victims, voiced the following at Dylann Storm Roof's court hearing: "I forgive you. You took something very precious away from me. I will never talk to her, ever again… but I forgive you, and have mercy on your soul … You hurt me. You hurt a lot of people. But God forgive you and I forgive you."[1]

In a world where shocking acts of violence and hatred force us to acknowledge the existence and presence of evil, we are occasionally and strangely challenged by examples that invite us to consider confronting evil by doing good. Just when the heavy darkness of the seemingly unforgivable is about to consume us and convince us to stay covered in the very darkness that suppresses us, the mysterious and miraculous light of forgiveness creeps slowly over the horizon. Despite the relief, direction and freedom that it brings, forgiveness is not welcomed by all. Some oppose forgiveness with the same vehemence with which the acts of evil were committed.

Although most of us have not been called upon at the arraignment of a someone who viciously took the life of someone we loved, we know on some level that the act of forgiving those who hurt us is very rarely, if ever, easy. So, I ask you, have you ever been hurt by someone you care about and struggled to forgive? I imagine everyone could answer that question with an emphatic YES! It's probably the very reason you are reading this book. What about being the one to have caused someone else's pain? If you take a few moments, you might even be able to remember what it was like to muster up the courage to say, "I am sorry" and hope for forgiveness. Here is the reality, we have all been there and, more importantly, we will all be there again as long as we choose to invest in significant relationships with other imperfect people.

To some, talking about good and evil sounds so intense and unreal but the heights and depths of our emotional experiences are just as intense and just as real. Where there are significant relationships, there will be significant hurt. If you value a relationship and want to move past deep hurts and terrible experiences in a healthy way, you will cross paths with forgiveness and reconciliation. One cannot effectively discuss or execute a Genuine Apology without navigating the topics of forgiveness and reconciliation. It is a sad truth that many people have just as much trouble discussing these topics as they do practicing them.

Apologies, forgiveness and reconciliation are so closely connected that some people are of the opinion that they are all basically the same and there's no real value in teasing or telling them apart. I have witnessed enough damaged and healed relationships to know that although apologies and forgiveness make good companions, they don't always travel together. I am also aware that many people assume that reconciliation is the defining mark of forgiveness and should automatically follow an apology. But, I disagree! There are significant differences between an apology, forgiveness, and reconciliation and blending these three concepts blurs the distinct roles each one plays in the healing and ongoing health of individuals and their relationships.

This chapter aims to make the power of a Genuine Apology accessible by delivering clarity and a deeper understanding of forgiveness and reconciliation and how they intersect with apologies. Together, we will discuss their similarities, highlight their differences and observe how a Genuine Apology weds them together in a life-giving way. Because we have already defined what an apology is and is not, let's delve into forgiveness.

WHAT IS FORGIVENESS?

The healing and restoration of countless relationships revolve around forgiveness. Many cherish their experiences of giving and receiving forgiveness and have come to see forgiveness as a value in and of itself. Yet, despite the endless instances of forgiveness, people still find it very hard to understand and execute. Alexander Pope's well know phrase "to err is human; to forgive, divine" acknowledges the fact that as humans we will make mistakes and wrong choices but we can transcend these very human experiences when we open ourselves to forgiveness. Very few will deny that we will all be in the position to forgive many times over the course of our lives but just as true is the reality that we will also be in need of an experience of forgiveness that can move us beyond the factual state of guilt and the unpleasant and painful emotions that tend to stay with us longer than we want them to.

When it comes to understanding forgiveness, there are several questions that most people hope to find answers to. Two of these questions include: If I forgive, will I feel better? And, how long should it take? The fading and eventual disappearance of unpleasant emotions like resentment and hatred are definitely a part of the process of forgiveness. If we are open and ready to forgive, it can happen immediately, but in some cases, it can take a long time to forgive. The amount of time it takes actually depends on you. Some people delay forgiving and hide behind the saying that "time heals all wounds", but I don't believe that saying is true at all. Forgiveness is a process that happens within time but requires more than the passing of time. In other words, time itself does not bring about forgiveness or the healing we desire.

Thinking about the process of healing in a physical sense can help us appreciate that time itself does not heal wounds. If our bodies are healthy, after sustaining an injury blood rushes to the area and the healing process begins. Although we don't see the inner workings of the process, our red blood cells are hard at work, producing collagen, fibers that build a foundation for new tissue which will eventually be covered by new skin. Healing involves work!

If the passing of time alone could heal our emotional wounds we could sit back, watch the clock and wait for forgiveness to spontaneously occur. That's not the way it happens. In fact, without intentional focus on forgiveness the passing of time can have the opposite effect and allow for increased hurt if we ruminate on the offence, recall other offenses and make things worse by considering ways to get revenge. What we do, and more importantly the thoughts we think after we've been hurt, will inform how much time forgiveness and healing takes. More specifically, how you interpret the situation, how you process hurt, the conclusions you come to and what you choose to do based on those conclusions will make all the difference in the world.

But what does forgiveness really involve? Can someone just say the words and presto, it's done? Similar to an apology going much deeper and much farther than saying "I am sorry", forgiveness is more than saying "I forgive you." While voicing these words is often a good place to start, if you really, I mean *really really* want to forgive someone for something that has impacted you deeply, it is important to come to terms with what you are forgiving.

While the journey is difficult the process is rather simple. You can forgive by labeling what was done as well as the impact that it had on you in the past, the present and the future. Take for example, a parent who has lost a child because someone chose to drive under the influence of a substance. The process and experience of forgiveness will entail overcoming the memory of the incident, enduring the current pain of daily reminders that their child is no longer with them as well as grieving the fact that they will not see their child grow up, become a grandparent or fulfill any of the dreams they had that involved that child. Even though forgiving in such situations seems impossible, it is important to remember that it is possible. My intent in spelling out what forgiving someone entails is not to make it seem easy. I am attempting to delineate a clear process because many people want to forgive and don't know where to begin.

When Nadine Collier, declared "God forgive you and I forgive you" her words expressed a reality that beyond the acknowledgment of her loss and pain at the hand of another existed a resolve and a strength to do the most difficult thing she would likely ever be asked to do.

Like many people around the world, her belief in God and the belief that God forgives made it both important and possible for her to do the same. Yet, many people who believe in God also struggle to forgive. Does that mean that you don't believe enough? Something is wrong with you? God is not helping you? Or that you are just not ready to forgive? I would argue that Nadine's specific beliefs and thoughts about forgiveness factor greatly into her experience and expression of forgiveness. Dissecting your beliefs about forgiveness is an integral part of forgiving.

What Do You Believe About Forgiveness?

Should forgiveness be easy or automatic and enduring? Your answers to these questions will reveal your beliefs about forgiveness and will directly inform your experience of accessing and offering forgiveness. Sometimes, even after having made attempts to forgive people are not able to believe they've really forgiven because feelings of anger, hatred and bitterness are still present or return from time to time. I have some good news for you, the return of old feelings does not indicate that you have not forgiven. Instead, it communicates the need to forgive again. Whether you chose to forgive in order to move forward or as a way to release someone from the guilt of their actions, in my experience, if the hurt is deep, you will be invited to forgive over and over again. I use the term "invited" as a way to see the positive side to a painful reality that forgiveness may require you to forgive a single offense many times.

Although it seems that the hurt party is expected to do all of the hard work for the sole benefit of the offender, this is not the case. The editor of this book, and my dear friend, Janice James-Brown, shared the words of Lewis B. Smedes with me, "To forgive is to set a prisoner free and discover that the prisoner was you." Forgiving others frees us from holding on to hatred, anger and bitterness, the very things that rob us of the freedom to experience joy and peace. There is no doubt in my mind that anger and resentment can prevent all of us from living the best life possible. Fortunately, each painful memory we recall can be used as an opportunity to promote healing in our lives.

For someone who has been hurt deeply, it is important to know that there are many kinds of invitations to forgive, most of which we cannot avoid. So, it is wise to try to make use of them when they come. Some unavoidable examples of invitations to forgive are visual, auditory and even olfactory reminders of the person or the incident. If you've ever experienced a significant breakup or loss you will be able to appreciate that many things will remind you of the person you are no longer in relationship with. Pictures, places, similar faces, songs, foods and fragrances are just a few examples.

Another invitation to forgive again is recognizing additional consequences connected to the situation and the person you've already forgiven. Take for example, discovering that there was more to the story that the person who hurt you didn't share. For instance, a devastated woman learns, not only was he unfaithful but he contracted an STI (sexually transmitted infection), which means she was exposed and will need to visit her doctor to ensure her health has not been compromised. Beyond the worrisome practical steps one would take in this kind of situation, we can also imagine how severely one's sense of trust in the nature of people and their own personal safety in this world could be shaken giving rise to hurtful memories and more invitations to forgive.

While these kinds of unpleasant and even painful invitations, whether brought about by reminders of the offence or new information compounding one's pain, could cause us to run away from them, it is important that we experience them and remind ourselves that life is not over. Viewing these reminders and invitations to forgive as a way to help you move forward and work through the pain that you're experiencing is difficult but possible. I can imagine someone saying, "I can't do this on my own!" You may be right. Thankfully, you don't have to. Whether you rely on God, family, friends or even a counsellor, there is help for you, if you are open to receiving it.

While receiving support seems logical, feelings of shame and even pride can stop us from accessing the help we know is necessary. A change of mind is often the deciding factor in making progress on this journey. Reflecting on the process of forgiveness helps us to see that it can involve a repeated changing of the mind; reminding ourselves of what we choose to believe when unhelpful thoughts cross our minds (i.e. *I can't forgive!* vs. *It is hard but I choose to forgive*). The continual correcting of thoughts will lead to a repeated change of heart and eventually, the releasing of bitterness and resentment.

In addition to letting go of bitterness and resentment, we can also release others from the burden of repayment. In some cases, repayment is appropriate, however, more important than the concrete repayment of a debt is the release of a desire for the other person to suffer. This is a very important part of the forgiveness process. If we find ourselves wanting someone to suffer, that is an indication that there is room for more forgiveness.

Similarities Between Forgiveness And Apologies

As noted earlier, forgiving others does so much more than absolve them of guilt, it releases the strong hold of anger, bitterness and resentment. Herein lies a similarity between forgiveness and apologies. Both the act of extending forgiveness and offering an apology can benefit the giver just as much as the receiver. Even though offering an apology does not absolve someone of responsibility, it can open the door for the hurt party to forgive and subsequently release the offending party from feelings of guilt. Both of these experiences can help the apology giver to feel a sense of pride and relief. The freedom that comes from knowing you've done all you can to address the hurt you've caused is priceless. This an important aspect of offering a Genuine Apology that people don't often see. Although we cannot control whether or not forgiveness is extended to us, when we offer a Genuine Apology, we are doing our part to make things right which can be a freeing experience.

Furthermore, the freedom obtained after offering a Genuine Apology is similar and often connected to the release that comes from forgiving one's self. While we often think of forgiveness being extended to others, forgiving ourselves is something that is also of great importance. Some people have lived beneath the weight of withheld forgiveness for years, however, there is a difference between accepting responsibility and enduring unrelenting guilt trips, insults and accusations. If you've apologized and asked for forgiveness and are waiting for forgiveness, the good news is, you don't have to wait forever. In the same sense that you can readily offer a Genuine Apology at your own volition and pace, you can forgive yourself whenever you'd like and do your best to move forward without repeating the offence or bludgeoning yourself until someone is ready to forgive you. Otherwise, you could be waiting for the rest of your life. And, that's no way to live!

Another similarity between a Genuine Apology and forgiveness is that the offering can be made as soon as you become aware of an infraction. You don't have to wait for someone to ask for forgiveness before giving it, nor do you have to wait for someone to ask you for an apology. As soon as you become aware of some sort of wrong doing on your part, seize the opportunity and apologize! As far as similarities between apologies and forgiveness go, that's the end of the line. Surprisingly, there are many more differences than there are similarities.

Differences Between Forgiveness And Apologies

While many scenarios feature the offering of an apology immediately followed by a request for forgiveness, they are different. They are literally two separate things that can function apart from each other. In some cases, usually in less intense situations, an apology will be offered without a request for forgiveness. In these instances, one may simply acknowledge their mistake or error in judgment, accept responsibility and not feel the need for forgiveness. For example, "I am sorry honey, dinner will be a little late, I was multi-tasking and lost track of time." This highlights that forgiveness and an apology are not simply the same thing with different names, they can, and often do, exist apart from each other.

As stated earlier, you don't have to wait for someone to ask for forgiveness before you offer it. Forgiveness does not require an apology or an acknowledgment of wrongdoing. We forgive when and because we choose to. The other person does not need to be sorry or deserving of it.

Forgiveness doesn't demand changes in another person or the offering of an apology. The truth is, even though we'd like people to acknowledge their wrongdoing before we forgive, we don't need them to. Forgiveness can happen without the person ever knowing that they were forgiven. And here is something even more fantastic! The offending party doesn't even need to be alive for you to forgive them. Many people who have been hurt by someone who has died experience a terribly complicated grieving process due to unexpressed grievances, unacknowledged hurts and withheld forgiveness. Yet on the other hand, the death or absence of an offending party can make forgiving that person a little easier because you don't have to worry about the person being wise enough or mature enough to acknowledge what you're saying without defensiveness or further risk of harm.

One of the most significant differences between apologizing and forgiving is the length of the process. Even though it may take time to come around to offering a Genuine Apology, generally speaking, it does not take a long time to be shared. Forgiveness, on the other hand, may require a lot more time to consider and experience all of the elements in the process as described earlier.

Both forgiveness and Genuine Apologies can, and likely will look different for each person and each situation, however, acknowledging the differences between apologizing and forgiving helps to offer some guidelines and set some limits.

While I do believe forgiving again and again is a good thing, even if only for our own healing, I do not believe apologizing again and again is necessary or helpful. A Genuine Apology is aimed at sufficiently addressing the hurts and meeting the needs of those we care about. In the case where a new hurt connected to a past event has been recently unveiled or someone tells you of a recent invitation to forgive you again, there is nothing wrong with offering another Genuine Apology, however, apologizing again and again, virtually on a daily basis for weeks and months on end often encourages people to stay in a victimized role and goes beyond validating their hurt to the point of supporting their choice not to forgive. Very few relationships can survive this dynamic.

I have one more difference to note. Unlike an appropriately scrutinized apology that is rightly accompanied by the expectation of trust to be earned after it has been broken, forgiveness is best given freely, no strings attached. If we wait for a demonstration of change to forgive, we may never forgive. I know this sounds scary to some because they want to know they will not endure the same hurts again and again before they forgive, but I believe they are confusing forgiveness with reconciliation. Let's dispel the confusion by defining what reconciliation really is.

WHAT IS RECONCILIATION?

If we picture forgiveness as the pardoning of an offense and releasing of the offender, reconciliation could be seen as the embracing of the offender. Not just a one-armed shoulder to shoulder hug followed by a double pat on the back, but a long embrace that leads to two people walking away from a hurtful situation hand in hand. Reconciliation is the reuniting of two people, coming together and re-engaging in a close, trusting, renewed and improved relationship. This requires change! A commitment to change is the heartbeat of reconciliation and healthy relationships require it! People may agree to get along after an offense and may even continue in a relationship without thoroughly addressing the offense and the drastic changes to be made, but I question how healthy that relationship is or will ever be.

Many relationships involve a cycle of hurt where people are committed to the value of forgiveness more than the health and integrity of their relationship. Idealistic phrases like "Forgive and forget" don't help us appreciate what reconciliation involves. Similarly, scriptural statements about forgiveness like, "forgive 70 times 7", "forgive us our debts as we forgive our debtors" or "do unto others as you would have them do unto you" are often used in relation to reconciliation. Unfortunately, when applied to reconciliation without adequate consideration about the agreement needed for two people to walk the road ahead, together, these words do more harm than good. In situations where people have been abandoned or abused in some way so that trust has been significantly broken, "I am sorry" is simply not good enough nor is "I forgive you" if your goal is true reconciliation.

One of my workshops about the art of a Genuine Apology addresses the reality that people *can* commit to and demonstrate change. Although all people, everywhere, and at all times, are eligible candidates for forgiveness, if they are not ready to commit to change and follow through, then they are not ready for reconciliation.

True reconciliatiotn involves making changes in order to move forward together. The proverb that questions whether or not two people can walk the same road without agreeing highlights a goal-oriented and a future-oriented perspective. If you want respect, honesty, trust, growth, health and healing as part of the relationship moving forward, changes in behavior is non-negotiable.

A ready candidate for reconciliation is someone that has undergone a change of heart and expresses this change of heart to the person he/she has hurt. When both parties want the same things and agree on how to achieve them, then reconciliation has begun. Agreement is paramount when it comes to reconciliation and it is the first difference between reconciliation and forgiveness that I want to bring light to.

Differences Between Forgiveness And Reconciliation

There are a couple of fundamental differences between forgiveness and reconciliation. Of these differences, agreement is the most critical. As noted earlier, forgiveness does not require agreement, but reconciliation does! With forgiveness, the emphasis and sole responsibility rests upon the hurt party who is choosing to forgive. Where forgiveness depends on one, reconciliation requires two. I can forgive someone whether or not they believe they are responsible for my pain or if they choose to change, it is all up to me. That is not the case for reconciliation. Before we can be reconciled, we must first agree on where we are going.

Reconciliation calls for both parties to participate. And, while joint participation will benefit both parties, unlike forgiveness the weight of change and responsibility lies most heavily on the offending party. Reconciliation's dependence on the offender vs. forgiveness being solely dependent on the offended is a pivotal difference. Just because you forgive someone does not mean they will change their ways. Unlike forgiveness, reconciliation cannot precede change, it always follows it.

While reconciliation is the ultimate destination, we cannot get there without sufficiently navigating forgiveness. Forgiveness and reconciliation do not share an equal or interchangeable relationship; the order cannot be reversed. Forgiveness will always precede reconciliation. Forgiveness can occur without reconciliation, however, without forgiveness, there can be no reconciliation.

Knowing these differences between forgiveness

and reconciliation, particularly the order in which they are experienced will prevent people from thinking they have been reconciled prematurely. Take for example the unfaithful partner who asks for forgiveness and has returned to the matrimonial home. This person might assume reconciliation has occurred because they are living in the same house again. However, even if the party who was betrayed agrees for the other to come home, that doesn't mean that they have any confidence for fidelity in the future. They might even be considering leaving the relationship out of spite or simply being "done."

Many couples stay together after hurtful experiences of betrayal. While they choose not to get divorced, one could argue that they have not been reconciled because forgiveness has not been given or experienced. Don't get me wrong, I am not pressuring anyone to forgive in order to be reconciled. I just want you to remember, offering forgiveness does not necessarily lead to being truly reconciled, it just needs to happen first.

Change is an integral part of reconciliation. While I am an advocate for forgiveness, I do not support giving someone license to continue to hurt you. Despite how helpful forgiving again and again can be, I want to be clear that offering forgiveness to the same person for the same or similar offences again and again is not the route to reconciliation. Even though the number of times one offers forgiveness can be limitless, it is important to recognize that forgiveness is not synonymous with reconciliation.

Beyond the fact that forgiveness precedes reconciliation, there is also great benefit to appreciating where someone is in the forgiveness process. Although reconciliation depends largely on the offending party choosing to change, their choice will not make a difference if the forgiveness process is not well underway. Before we can reconcile, we must not only agree on where we are going, but understand the impact of what we've gone through. Just because someone forgives doesn't mean they are ready for reconciliation. Similarly, just because someone apologizes does not mean they are ready for reconciliation either.

Differences Between An Apology And Reconciliation

While an apology is a good place to start, an apology is not reconciliation. Just because someone sincerely apologizes does not mean that they will do whatever it takes not to hurt you again. While it is a step in the right direction, in most cases it is one step of many that are to be taken in order to be ready for reconciliation. If your journey to forgiveness was thorough and involved a deep awareness of the impact the other person's actions have had, you will be keenly aware of how your life has changed. Not only will you be acquainted with pain in a new way, but you will see the situation in a more comprehensive light. It is just as important that the person you want to be reconciled with understands how your life and your perspective has changed. A simple or common apology does not guarantee that someone has undergone the changes necessary for reconciliation.

When someone understands your pain and your perspective, they will appreciate the time and effort rebuilding your trust may require. An ability to express this degree understanding is another indication of readiness for reconciliation. Simply saying "I am sorry" does not demonstrate the understanding required to be ready for reconciliation.

Even if forgiveness is requested and granted after an apology this doesn't mean that you have to or even should re-engage on the same relational level with the person who hurt you. Just because you offer forgiveness doesn't mean that you have been or should be immediately reconciled to the other person. If the perspective of the person you want to be reconciled with doesn't change then you will likely experience the same or similar hurts in that relationship again whether or not their apology was sincere.

I know this is a lot to take in, but it is imperative that we know what we are really saying when we use the words forgiveness and reconciliation. Now that we've discussed the differences between apologies, forgiveness and reconciliation, we are ready to see how they all fit together.

TYING FORGIVENESS, APOLOGIES AND RECONCILIATION TOGETHER

It is my desire to encourage each and every individual reading this book to experience healing in their most significant relationships through the giving and receiving of Genuine Apologies, forgiveness and reconciliation. When we have a good understanding of the differences between them we can be more intentional about when and how to engage in them.

At any given time, one can offer forgiveness without the offender accepting responsibility, however, reconciliation (re-engaging in a close, renewed and improved relationship) requires that the offending party truly understand the impact their actions have had on the other person. This understanding will lead to a commitment to change which is best communicated with a Genuine Apology.

Remember, not every apology is a "Genuine Apology". Even a sincere and meaning-full apology doesn't necessarily communicate readiness for reconciliation. In relationships where hurt or abuse are routine, you will likely find endless apologies and extended forgiveness, however, these apologies and these relationships are missing key ingredients that bring about true reconciliation. These key ingredients are the very same values woven into a Genuine Apology. Whether abusive or not, in most hurtful situations, a common apology extends a request for forgiveness but rarely acknowledges the extent of the hurt caused. A Genuine Apology, that incorporates the steps laid out in the remainder of this book can be used to assess readiness for reconciliation, and can tie forgiveness and reconciliation together in a powerful and meaningful way.

Let's imagine significant distance exists between you and a loved one as a result of hurtful choices. When we offer a Genuine Apology, we are building a bridge between ourselves and that person. If we have created the distance, building this bridge is our responsibility. It may take time and hard work, but it humbly demonstrates our love and commitment to the other person. The level of vulnerability, sincerity and accountability built into the bridge speaks to the integrity and strength of the bridge and can give the other person confidence to attempt coming across the bridge we've built.

The reality is, no matter how good a bridge you or I build, the other person gets to decide whether or not they will take the chance to cross it, forgive us and be reconciled with us. Similarly, if someone has built a bridge for you to cross, it would be wise to inspect it before running across it with all of your might only to find that it was incomplete, riddled with holes or simply not strong enough to support all of the wonderful things you desire to bring to the relationship.

When humility, vulnerability, empathy, responsibility and accountability are a part of an apology, we can truly see how it can serve as a bridge between forgiveness and reconciliation. Regardless of how hurt you have been, I believe that giving and receiving forgiveness coupled with assessing readiness for reconciliation by way of a Genuine Apology, allows you to come out on the other side better than how you went in.

In the chapters ahead we will examine 4 steps to building a Genuine Apology. You can use these steps to build "bridges" of your own as well as assess when to move beyond forgiveness and into reconciliation. But before we start building bridges, let's solidify what we've discussed by reflecting on the questions below.

For your consideration

1. How often do you forgive?
2. Do you find forgiving others difficult?
3. Is it easy to forgive yourself?
4. How do you define reconciliation?
5. Have you forgiven someone and assumed both of you were ready for reconciliation only to have a pattern repeat itself?
6. Is there someone you want to forgive, apologize to or be reconciled with?

Now that we've discussed how a Genuine Apology can aid crossing over from forgiving to being reconciled you may be inspired to forgive, assess readiness for reconciliation and offer a Genuine Apology, but before you attempt giving your apology, I want you to be aware of several things that could derail your efforts.

---

1. [CNN]. (2015, June 19).Victims' relatives forgive, urge shooter to repent [Video File]. Retrieved from https://youtu.be/cIRcGwBrdbE

CHAPTER EIGHT

Spoiler Alert!

Have you ever started to offer an apology only to have the other person become even more upset and leave you wondering, *"Now what did I say!?"* Or have you ever been on the receiving end of an apology that started off well only to become turned off at some point during the delivery and convinced the person was insincere? Wouldn't it be great if, in one of those moments of spoiling a perfectly good apology, someone could hold up a warning *"Spoiler alert!"* sign? Ok, perhaps that is a bit silly, but here is the reality; the experience of a spoiled apology is not at all uncommon. It's actually tragic. While I have successfully helped some to avoid ruining priceless moments, I have watched many sincere attempts at apologies crash and burn right in front of me.

In some cases, people can look back and see what they did to ruin their apologies but in the majority of cases, people have absolutely no idea of what went wrong. Being able to recognize, and help someone else recognize, when they are ruining an apology, is one of the most important benefits of learning the art of a Genuine Apology. Words are indeed powerful and so, it is absolutely essential to be aware of what words, phrases and attitudes can destroy a Genuine Apology and how to avoid them. In this chapter, we will explore some of the most common apology spoilers and how to stay away from them.

Using The Word 'But'

I would dare say that using the word 'but' in an apology is the most common way to ruin and nullify an apology. Time and time again, I hear someone offer an apology and as soon as they say the word 'but' I see a range of emotions, from mild irritation to intense disgust, flash across the face of the once again, hurt, receiving party. Now why do you think that is? The answer is actually very simple. The word 'but' cancels out everything that came before it! 'But' is a conjunctive word tying two statements together, but it simultaneously contrasts the two, often placing emphasis on the latter statement, the portion following the 'but'.

It's reasonable to think that most people use 'buts' in

their apologies because they are unaware or simply don't see the harm in it. However, even after reading about the impact of using 'but' in an apology, I know many people are thinking, *Hmmmm... Drew, there are some times when a 'but' is a valid point to make! What if the reason you now have to apologize is because you were provoked? Or, if you are apologizing for a situation that was not your fault?!* Ah yes, I have encountered these questions and experienced many of these situations before. In fact, in the past, I have perpetrated some of them myself.

As humans dealing with other humans, there will be many situations that seem 'but' worthy. Take for example two people in a disagreement and one, sensing it is going too far, sincerely tries to stop it by offering the following apology, "I am sorry. I hate arguing with you, but sometimes you make me so angry!" In the less than two seconds it takes to utter the word 'but', what you have done is given an apology, taken it back and assigned blame to the other person. Now the disagreement has escalated.

You see, regardless of what you intend to convey, from the hearer's perspective, when you say, "I'm sorry but…" you are actually not sorry. How it reads is that you are abdicating your responsibility and placing blame. And although you may not intend to disregard the other person's feelings and place the blame on them, this is precisely what people hear when we use the word 'but' in our apologies

In my experience, individuals who opt to use the "I am sorry, but..." style of apology are those who feel their actions were warranted and want to make a point. Parent's of teens often find themselves in this position, however, regardless of how important your point is, it will fall on deaf ears if your apology is accompanied by a 'but'.

Before racing off to tell someone about their 'buts' I want you to be prepared. If it is brought to their attention they will likely try to share their reasons for using it, which could cause you to believe they are not sorry at all. I don't want you to come to this conclusion too quickly. It is important to be able to tolerate the defensiveness and unintentional hurts we experience in order to receive clarity about the messages they intend to send. It is also a great opportunity to lovingly teach them how to interact with us differently. Understanding the people we love will help us to be understanding with them. So, let's look at some of the logical reasons people use the word 'but' when attempting to apologize.

The Defensive 'But'

Have you ever spoken to someone who is on the defensive? And no matter what you say to them, they have a quick reply, justifying their actions? Do they simply believe they have to be right all of the time? Maybe they do, or, perhaps attaching a 'but' to their apology is a quick way to defend themselves. In one sense, every 'but' can be seen and experienced as defensive, however, sometimes people are not trying to be right or defend their actions, they are simply trying to guard against feelings of guilt and shame. Sometimes people respond with a defensive 'but' if they feel awkward and simply want a way out. Being caught by surprise or being unprepared for a confrontation where an apology is expected of them can also be a reason people use the word 'but' alongside their apology.

Although you may have heard or used many defensive 'buts', I want to list the ones I've come across so you can both avoid using them and anticipate their use by others. Keep an eye out for the 'buts' used to justify one's actions, they usually sound like this, "I am sorry, but you make me so angry" or "I am sorry but you hurt me too!" I have also heard, "I am sorry but if you didn't... then I wouldn't have to..."

Then, there are the insensitive 'buts', "I am sorry

that you feel that way, but..." or "I am sorry if I hurt your feelings but...." As you read these examples you are probably reminded that they don't sound like and wouldn't feel like apologies at all. So, for your sake and for the sakes of those you love, please avoid using a 'but' in your apologies.

Offering An Explanation

Like peanut butter and jelly (or jam if you are Canadian), 'but' often has a companion, an explanation. Have you ever experienced an apology with an explanation following a 'but'? I'm sure you have. You may have served an explanation on the side of your apology once or twice before. I think we all have, once or twice... maybe three... thousand times. While it may make perfectly logical sense in everyday conversations to share your perspective on how a situation came to be, it does not have the same effect in the context of an apology. Unless you are explaining how you will fix the problem you are responsible for, marrying an apology with an explanation is the antithesis of a Genuine Apology and will, in all likelihood, sound like an excuse.

When you say "sorry" and then validate your actions with an explanation, you are simultaneously dismissing the other person's experience. Even if your explanation is not just an excuse it is important to be aware that offering it will likely leave the hearer feeling jilted and yield unpleasant results. If people feel dismissed by your apologies they may tune you out and even lose respect for you. This can happen immediately but can also happen over time if explanations are routinely a part of your apologies. It's also worth noting that offering an explanation as part of your apology can prevent you from adequately accepting responsibility and changing your behavior, which doesn't benefit you or the person you are apologizing to.

Is it possible to offer an explanation with an apology without it sounding like an excuse? The short answer is Yes, it is possible. A more complete answer is that while it is possible it is also very tricky and will depend on two things: 1) whether the situation was totally beyond your control and 2) the degree of hurt experienced by the person you are apologizing to. If there was absolutely no way to have done something differently acknowledging that in your apology may not upset the other person. However, even if that is the case, it is still a big risk to take because without them telling you, it's impossible to know exactly how hurt someone actually is. If they are deeply hurt, it is likely that your reason won't matter at all and will sound like an excuse or laying of blame. Thus, my advice is to hold off on the explanations even when they may seem reasonable.

"It Was A Mistake!"

I want to address a line that appears in some of the worst apologies I have ever heard, "I'm sorry... it was a mistake!" Here is a similar line, used more frequently by children and teens, "It was an accident!" Both of these statements are terribly disappointing and often very inaccurate. The term accident is appropriate when there was no intention to carry out the action that hurt or offended the other person. Similarly, a mistake acknowledges an error in judgment. For example, if you and I have identical phones and I didn't look for distinguishing marks and picked up the wrong one, that would qualify as a simple mistake or something done accidentally. HOWEVER, there is a big difference between making a mistake and making a bad decision.

While both a mistake and a bad decision may lead to an apology, mistakes are unintentional and can happen to anyone, whereas, bad decisions are choices that we actually give thought to (albeit insufficient thought). The accepted phenomenon of people labeling their choice to be unfaithful as a mistake will forever puzzle me.

Making Light Of The Situation

That last comment might lead one to think that I don't appreciate how difficult it is to acknowledge one's errors. I totally get it and I don't mean to make light of such a horrible experience, however, it is important for everyone to refuse to be satisfied with people shirking their responsibilities. Some people use words like "mistake" or "accident" to moderate the potential backlash of the person they've hurt and others intentionally attempt to ease the tension with a joke or resort to paying compliments in hopes of mesmerizing the wounded hearted. This might be cute, once or twice and it may have even become a part of your natural way of being, however, over time, being unable to convey serious, somber and mature sentiment can drive a wedge between you and those you care about.

Regardless of your intentions, or your awareness, most people who have been hurt or offended will likely consider addressing the issue to be very serious and worthy of sober consideration. A comical response in a hurtful situation can feel like a slap in the face and will likely make the person feel more hurt and angry. If people don't get the sense that you can be serious, they will not trust that you will be capable of managing serious situations and make the changes that matter to them.

Nonverbal Communication

Another too often overlooked way to ruin an apology comes through our nonverbal communication. Nonverbal communication includes posture, eye contact, facial expressions, proximity to the person as well as the tone and volume of our voices. It is critical that we remain aware that our apologies are augmented by what we do, how we look and how we sound when we deliver them. I mentioned the litany earlier "It's not what you say, but how you say it". Although it definitely applies here, when it comes to increasing the effectiveness of one's apology, I would add to that statement, "It's not what you say but how you say it. But don't forget, it all comes down to how it is perceived."

Awareness of our nonverbal communication is especially relevant for those of you who find expressing feelings hard and dealing with conflict next to impossible, because in such moments you might have a nervous smile on your face. If you are the party offering the apology, and you are aware that when feeling awkward or nervous you might smile or laugh, it is best to mention that to the person you want to apologize to before beginning your apology. It is hard to change this kind of involuntary behavior immediately, but most people will be understanding about it, providing the rest of the exchange contains the necessary elements to make it a Genuine Apology.

Beware Of Gifts!

Under normal circumstances, most people enjoy receiving gifts. However, as a strategy to avoid facing unpleasant emotions, conflicts or the consequences of harmful actions, giving gifts has been employed as a way to placate, deflect and render moot any wrongdoing. This strategy, observed in media as well as in real life family dramas, has been used for a number of infractions from missed birthdays to anniversaries or as a general "get out of jail free card" in lieu of an actual apology for decades and maybe even centuries. Whether you don't know what to do, are at a loss for words or never have been great with words, simply buying a gift is still taking the easy way out! While the intention may be to say sorry, impact someone's mood or redeem the warm tone of the relationship, gifts can also be a distraction from the issues that are important for you to address.

Bad Timing

Apologizing well involves worthwhile consideration of your choice of words, your body language as well your timing. While apologizing as soon as possible is in keeping with the spirit of bringing healing to our most significant relationships it is important to bear in mind that some moments are less effective than others to offer an apology. I don't want to dissuade you from apologizing, but it is very important to know that a poorly timed apology can impact the person you're apologizing to just as negatively as if the apology was followed by an explanation or wrapped in a joke. Even if we want to be responsible and are sincerely remorseful, choosing the wrong timing can illustrate that, once again, we are not being thoughtful about what is best for the other person.

This aspect of offering an apology can be very tricky because, along with the timing of when an apology is offered, it is just as important to think about the context and setting in which we offer the apology. As an example, apologies are often shared in private because most people prefer to keep vulnerable experiences to themselves so, offering a Genuine Apology about a private situation in a public setting usually doesn't go over well. However, if the hurtful event occurred in the presence of others, it may well warrant an immediate public apology, followed by another one in private.

Ok Drew, I get what you are saying, but how do I know if the timing is right? I understand it may be hard to know if the timing is right and how to avoid being a gift or 'but' giving apologizer so, below are some tips on what to look for and how to avoid apology spoilers.

For your consideration

Back To The 'Buts'

So, what are you to do if you are not entirely to blame for a situation? Is a 'but' leading to an explanation appropriate then? The short answer is… No! Here's why. Even though a 'but' is a totally legitimate conjunction in day to day circumstances, it is not usually the most helpful strategy when there has been an argument, someone is hurting or when tensions are high and you have any part to play in the situation. If you do not believe it is right, fair or helpful to take responsibility for the entire situation but recognize that even a small part of the situation was caused by your actions the best thing to do is acknowledge your part and apologize for it.

Specifically stating that you are taking responsibility for your part makes it abundantly clear that there is room for others to take responsibility without blaming them or using a 'but'. Your statement could look something like this, "I know when I responded to your comment about my family's issues I was feeling irritated and I raised my voice and left the room. I apologize for raising my voice and leaving the conversation before entirely hearing your perspective."

This response allows the other person to see you taking responsibility for your part. It also silently invites them to examine the entire situation, follow suit and take responsibility. Now, it is possible that they may not see it the way you do and follow suit with an apology of their own. So, it is important to be okay with this because you cannot dictate the timing of someone acknowledging and accepting responsibility for their choices. You can only manage and be responsible for yours.

Strings Attached

As intimated earlier, gifts can be a sincere attempt to apologize and make things better but they can also be attempts to smooth things over and sweep things under the rug. It's important to know the difference so that you can avoid unwittingly upsetting the other person when you're apologizing and avoid letting the perpetrator off the hook when receiving an apology. If you happen to be on the receiving end of a gift and are unsure about the intention, you can simply ask. Acceptance of a gift without clarification about the giver's intent could be experienced as forgiving or excusing the behavior that precipitated the gift. If there seems to be a pattern of gifts following conflict, this may simply be a learned behavior that can be interrupted by acknowledging the pattern and/or refusing the gift.

Gift Giving And Its Role In Abusive Relationships

Because this kind of cycle often happens in abusive relationships, it is important to note that refusing the gift can also intensify the conflict and lead to further aggression so be cautious in how you manage this conversation and interaction. As noted at the beginning of this book, if you're experiencing abuse in your relationship I recommend speaking with a trained supportive professional about what you're experiencing. Experiencing positive change in abusive situations is more likely to happen when you have adequate support.

Timing Is Everything

We don't always know what time or what approach will work best, which can leave us feeling even more apprehensive about apologizing. Many conversations with people who really want to apologize has taught me that feeling unsure about when to apologize is reason enough to avoid apologizing. There are several things to both avoid and look for that can help determine when the timing is right to offer an apology.

1. Avoid Apologizing When The Recipient Is Busy

While this might seem like a no-brainer piece of

advice, after a hurtful exchange people tend to avoid each other and make themselves "busy" so it may be a little difficult to know if the person is legitimately busy or simply trying to avoid you. The best course of action is to let the person know that you'd like to offer an apology and ask if that moment is a good time for it. This approach is often experienced as respectful and leads people to being more receptive.

2. Avoid Apologizing When The Person Is Still Visibly Angry, Enraged Or Extremely Emotional

This may seem like a contradiction to some of the other advice found in this book, but I guarantee you it's not. Have you ever tried to have a conversation with an irate, enraged or heart-broken person? If so, you know how impossible it can be to get through to them. If the person you have hurt or angered is still in the newness of this experience, they might not want to be in your presence. If the individual you want to apologize to has expressed a desire for time and space away from you or the moment itself appears to need time to calm down, as a general rule, it's best to give the time and space requested. However, if the person tends to avoid conflict or sensitive issues or if you're about to be apart from each other for an extended period of time, it can be helpful to acknowledge the need for space as well as offer a brief apology with a commitment to return to it later.

If you have a specific time that you imagine will work for the two of you, state it, and be sure to follow through. If something urgent comes up, connect with them and reschedule. Although life may be full for you, be sure to make the time to follow up and avoid rescheduling where possible because your credibility is on the line.

3. Avoid Apologizing When You're Too Angry To Be Respectful

Generally, I'd agree that the sooner one apologizes the better, however, if you're feeling very angry and have not had a lot of experience managing your anger and maintaining respectful composure this would not be the time to attempt the full version of your Genuine Apology. More likely than not it will just come off all wrong. Instead, I recommend you keep the conversation, and apology, brief and return to it when you'll be more successful at using the strategies discussed throughout this book.

4. Define The Best Context In Which To Apologize

As mentioned earlier, this can be quite challenging. The trickiest apologies tend to be the ones where the offence occurred in the presence of others, especially children. More often than not, multiple apologies are warranted. In most cases a quick immediate public apology, both to the hurt party and the observers is best followed by a more thorough and private one. If the private one goes over well, it can be followed by a discussion about how you'd like to address the witnesses of the incident in order to see if the offended party is ready for this.

If the person is not open to another public apology for sheer embarrassment and wanting to leave the incident in the past, I recommend letting that person know that you desire to acknowledge the situation and the impact you may have had on others.

Discussing your intentions and your plans with the person you have hurt is very important, because they could experience additional hurt and embarrassment if the parties want to know more about how the hurt person is responding and you are not prepared or have not received permission to comment. Give it some thought prior to meeting with the person you have hurt and let that person know what you intend to say and when you intend to say it.

I want to dispel the myth that children don't require apologies. On the contrary, children are much more impressionable than adults. Even though they are more forgiving, the impact of witnessing unhealthy and hurtful interactions between parents and/or family members can shape their interactions with others, their perspective of you and what they believe about the world they live in. Countless children have grown to believe that being disrespectful to the people they love when they are hurt is acceptable and unavoidable. While they may view the more aggressive parent as the one to blame, these same children often have very little respect for both parents. It is important to give adequate thought to what you choose to revisit with an apology or leave alone with the hope that it will all be forgotten. Even if you have a hard time deciding, at least you can feel good about having had a discussion about it.

Now that we've reviewed what you can do to avoid things that can spoil your apology, let's give attention to the things that might be getting in the way of people apologizing to you.

CHAPTER NINE

Sticks and Stones

As a kid I was lead to believe that repeating the old adage "Sticks and stones may break my bones but words will never hurt me" would shield me from the terrible sting of grade school bullies and ward off further verbal attacks. Unfortunately, nothing could be further from the truth. As I think of the many clients I help to overcome historic and present-day experiences of being bullied and the internalized messages they've listened to for years, I am reminded that words can build up or break down one's spirit.

Although the first instances of damaging messages are usually words from parents, caregivers and peers, they eventually become our own and venture beyond our conscious thoughts, seeping deep into the realm of our beliefs. Our beliefs form the foundation of every single thing we say and do. They inform how we interpret situations and dictate how we feel. You see, our beliefs, our emotions, our lives are based on words. Words are indeed powerful.

Thankfully, the words we use can also bring healing to our lives and the lives of the people we love. Yet with all of this power at the tip of our tongues, we often remain silent, refusing to address the hurts we've caused. But why???? Many people find themselves refusing to apologize and don't really know the deeper reasons why. That's the question this chapter will address.

Far too many people find themselves stuck in patterns of hurt and confusion, engaging in unfruitful interactions when a Genuine Apology could change things drastically. The reasons and excuses we cite for refusing to apologize are like sticks and stones. Unlike words used to inflict hurt directly, our reasons and excuses hurt us indirectly. They construct barriers in our relationships, emotionally barricading us in and locking others out.

I have encountered many barriers to Genuine Apologies in my personal life and have been introduced to some new ones over the course of my professional practice. Whether they were built over time or overnight these barriers are made out of sticks and stones taken from the following five categories: intense and unpleasant emotions, pride, problematic beliefs, unhelpful attitudes and family patterns. In hopes of increasing our awareness of these sticks and stones as well as learning how to break down these mental and emotional barriers let's become more familiar with each of these categories.

Intense And Unpleasant Emotions

Years ago, I was working with a father who knew that he had made many decisions over the years that negatively impacted his 17-year-old daughter and their relationship. At that point in time, their communication had gone from routine arguments to sporadic and superficial conversations at best with months of silence in between. It was obvious that there were many things he could apologize for, however, his fears of causing and experiencing more hurt and disappointment produced great anxiety and distress.

As you might presume, if someone is actually guilty of hurting or offending another person, feelings like guilt, shame, self-hatred or embarrassment can be terribly hard to tolerate. The fear and pain associated with these unpleasant emotions can be enough to cause one to avoid situations or deny the existence of certain problems all together. In short, some people avoid apologizing to escape feeling intense and unpleasant emotions, but a Genuine Apology encourages you to tolerate and tunnel through these emotions. Although experiencing anxiety and distress are not the goal of this process it is of inestimable value to recognize that such emotions are barriers that can be overcome.

The first step in overcoming emotional barriers is realizing that feeling these kinds of emotions can in fact be healthy and helpful. *Drew, how on earth could you say that terrible emotions like distress and anxiety are healthy or helpful?* In my estimation, an indicator of emotional health is the ability to experience a wide range of emotions, including the unpleasant ones. It is just as important to be able to feel sad as it is to feel happy. So, yes, it is very healthy to be able to feel anxious and distressed. We tend to label these kinds of emotions as terrible, negative or just plain ol' bad based on how they cause us to feel physiologically. Even though experiencing particular emotions may not be enjoyable, they are neither good or bad.

Instead of labeling emotions as good or bad I describe them as pleasant or unpleasant for two reasons. First, it is not helpful to judge one's emotions. The terms good or bad connote right or wrong and I strongly encourage people to avoid judging their emotions or the emotions of others. The second reason tends to follow the first, to promote reflection and understanding. If we judge our feelings (or the feelings of others) as right or wrong, we will be more likely to avoid them, which naturally lends to missed opportunities to reflect on our emotions intentionally. The avoidance of thinking carefully about our emotions only makes situations worse.

Instead of judging our emotions, we stand to benefit greatly when we seek to understand them, logically. If you think about it this way, emotions are either appropriate for the situation or not. Let's take the unpleasant experiences surrounding death, for example. If someone close to you dies, it makes sense to feel loss and sadness, however, if in this scenario the person waged a terrible battle with cancer and you reflect on the fact that this person is no longer suffering and also believe that this person will now forever be in heavenly bliss, it can also make sense to be filled with joy. Understanding the thoughts attached to your emotions will help to appreciate them in their given context. It would not be helpful or fair to judge how you or anyone is feeling without understanding the context along with the accompanying thoughts and beliefs.

Being aware of our thoughts and possessing the ability to understand our emotions helps us to skillfully navigate challenging moments. It also helps us to be more patient with others. Thinking our way through emotional situations can be very rewarding as well as affirming, but be sure not to become cocky about your emotional intelligence. Despite how successful we become at experiencing and navigating the range of thoughts and emotions we experience, let's not assume that it will be or should be equally feasible for everyone else.

While, it is true in most cases that our thoughts fuel our emotions and our emotions stimulate physiological experiences, I don't want to oversimplify the human experience of emotions and conclude that it is the same for everyone and will be the same in every situation. I have learned that even though the intensity of our emotions is fairly consistently informed by our thoughts, the way we experience emotions as well as the intensity of the emotions in our bodies can vary drastically from one person to another. While two people may feel depressed about the same situation, not only can one person feel more depressed than the other, but someone might find feeling depressed terribly unbearable, literally painful to their bodies to the point of debilitation. If you haven't had this kind of experience or tend not to feel your emotions as intensely as others, it may be hard to refrain from being judgmental, however, judging someone else because of how they feel is hurtful and tends to make situations worse.

In short, we are never in a position to judge what someone else is experiencing because we are not in their bodies. Furthermore, being judgmental towards others will likely cause the other person to feel angry or ashamed, which in turn builds additional barriers for them to overcome.

Here is the crux of the matter with regard to intense or unpleasant emotions; while avoiding them is a typical human response, it only serves to mask and aggravate matters. I am convinced that working through issues, and the associated pain, is the only way to make things better. Accepting this reality can help us take action. I can't guarantee a positive outcome for each person, couple or family who chooses to work through their issues, especially if those you are interacting with are not open to engaging in a mutually responsible way, but I can say, that I have observed people experiencing incredible changes in their lives and in their relationships when they turn and face their issues head on instead of running away from them or pretending they don't exist. Living in denial doesn't help things in the long run. Nothing in life remains the same for long, that includes our problems. If we don't address them, they will likely get worse.

If you're feeling stuck, I hope that you will take the time to consider your options, because we always have options. One of the options is taking the time to learn to manage your emotions well, whether through activities like journaling, prayer or meeting with a counsellor. People who acknowledge their struggle with experiencing unpleasant emotions and choose to acquire the skills to manage them grow immensely and are better able to address their issues. They end up having richer and more fulfilling relationships.

Pride - One Presentation, Two Different Issues

Whether we are talking about challenges with experiencing and managing unpleasant emotions or repeated unwise choices in our interactions with others, unless we admit that there are things that we can do better our relationships will suffer. A refusal to acknowledge room for growth often indicates the presence of pride.

Some people actually believe they are better or smarter than others and are always right, while some people simply feel the need to be right. Regardless of what one thinks or how they feel, the reality is no one can be right all of the time because no one is perfect. We all have flaws and imperfections. Instead of delving into understandings of the origins of pride I will share my simple definition of it: pride can be defined as blindness to one's own imperfections. Some people are genuinely blind to their imperfections while others put blinders on. I like to refer to the latter form of blindness as camouflaged insecurity.

Many people walk through life unaware of the cost they pay for being blinded by pride. Whether one is keeping others at a distance because they believe they are better than others or are afraid of being hurt or rejected by others, pride gets in the way of apologizing and spells disaster for relationships. If someone is unable to see that they are capable of being wrong, they will naturally blame the other person when things are not going well. It's pretty easy to recognize this kind of pride because this won't be a single or occasional occurrence, it will happen consistently and with practically all of the people they interact with. I am not being over dramatic; I mean 99.999% of the time. Many people describe those who find it this hard to apologize as narcissistic. Fortunately, this kind of pride in its most extreme form does not occur as often as we tend to think.

Even though most people do not experience pride to this extreme, it is important to see how dangerously unhealthy this form of pride is and to detect it before you commit. If you observe this pattern in the life of someone you are considering marriage with, think about what your future will be like. It is definitely not an ingredient for the making of a happy and healthy relationship. If on the other hand, someone demonstrates the ability to acknowledge their mistakes and wrong decisions but tends to have a hard time apologizing then a prideful presentation is usually an indication that he or she is feeling insecure or trying to avoid being vulnerable. For some people, refusing to apologize is the last stand before they feel stupid, embarrassed, powerless and even useless. This takes us back to our discussion earlier about tolerating unpleasant emotions.

Insecurity And Unfair Expectations

With camouflaged insecurity under the guise of pride, some people effectively guard themselves against unpleasant feelings that are usually attached to strongly held beliefs. These beliefs often lend to individuals upholding unrealistic expectations of themselves and others. Let's look at an example of what I mean. Let's say that, as the "man of the house" I believe that I should be the one to make and manage all of the decisions around finances. Now let's imagine my wife suggests a strategy that is far better than mine. As a man who is insecure in my abilities, but too proud to admit it, I might have a number of responses: pretend as if I already knew her solution and was on the verge of implementing it, dismiss her solution as ineffective or ill-advised, or at the most self-preserving end of these options, I question her intelligence for suggesting such a solution.

Clearly, these reactions are fueled by insecurity shrouded with pride. Allowing myself to overlook valuable insight and discount my wife's acumen in this area would all be to avoid feeling less of a man because I was not the one to introduce the idea. All of this grounded in the belief that *I have to come up with the best ideas in order to be a man* or *a real man knows more than his wife about everything.* Now, from the outside, this may look silly to some, but to others, this may have set off bells! That's because this train of thought is more common than most of us (men) would like to admit. But while this particular example may be most common among men, this version of pride is not limited to men or finances.

Both men and women can occupy many roles in today's society. Unfair expectations of themselves and others can be attached to each and every role. Regardless of the role or situation, sustaining unrealistic expectations, which are essentially unhealthy beliefs, put an enormous amount of pressure on individuals as well as those they care about. The idea that men are not supposed to feel or express sadness or hurt is an example, still upheld by many people. Attempting to live up to such unrealistic expectations and trying to avoid feeling vulnerable only leaves people standing alone with the illusion of being strong, which at the end of the day is literally nothing to feel proud about.

Even in more seemingly progressive societies, many women expect to manage their homes, their jobs, their kids, their car and their health without help from anyone. Missing a beat and having one hair out of place would be an admission of failure or would leave a blemish on the title of admirable women gone before. Obviously, I am not a woman, but I am quite familiar with the unhealthy expectations that lead many women to become anxiety-ridden. Unrealistic expectations induce anxiety and increase insecurity within one's self and does a number on relationships. Healthy relationships are authentic relationships that revolve around realistic expectations. Realistic expectations give credence to the reality that we are imperfect which humbly, and wisely, gives rise to a willingness to apologize when you've done wrong.

Problematic Beliefs

One of the most unfortunate yet common beliefs attached to offering an apology, or more accurately, withholding one, is that apologizing is a sign of weakness. All-or-nothing beliefs like these invite us to accept the statement entirely or totally disagree with it. The reality is, in some cases, this statement may be very true and absolutely untrue in others. How can apologizing be a sign of weakness? If people fear conflict and/or have been conditioned to accept blame or responsibility, when conflict arises they tend to automatically apologize. Sometimes, this kind of apology has no conscious thought involved, while other times, the person might berate themselves, calling themselves names during and long after the interaction is over.

This kind of default apology can literally be a sign pointing to a weakness. This sort of response to situations leaves people of all ages vulnerable to bullies (don't forget adults can be bullies too). It also reveals that this person is not accessing their true strength. Notice that I did not say this person is weak or has no strength, they simply may not be aware that they have the strength to deal with conflict or know how to call upon that strength in that particular moment.

It is a terrible tragedy that some people will live and communicate from a position of inferiority for the rest of their lives. Whether those who apologize by default were taught to do so by hurtful experiences or simply have not had enough positive experiences advocating for themselves, the tragedy of living below their potential remains. Don't get me wrong, I am not declaring that you or anyone else will lead a life of inferiority for automatically saying, "Oh, I'm sorry" in simple situations, like most Canadians do. I am simply highlighting my belief that it is healthy to be able to *choose* to apologize as opposed to an apology being your typical or only response when conflicts or challenges arise, especially in your most significant relationships.

When someone chooses to apologize, it can be a sign of great strength. People who shy away from accepting responsibility are simultaneously refusing to be open to growth and are actively shutting down opportunities to bring healing to the people they love, making their relationships weaker. Choosing to acknowledge one's errors and apologize demonstrates that someone is brave enough to acknowledge their imperfections and accept that they have room to grow.

Yes, there is a chance that your decision to apologize will be seized, used as a trophy and revisited in future arguments, but this has more to do with the character of the person you are apologizing to. Yes, we will be in relationships with all sorts of people who will be at various points in their development, however, you can decide how close you will be with others every day. If someone is a danger to you emotionally, I encourage you to love them from a safe distance and reserve your vulnerability for when they will cherish it.

Unhelpful Attitudes

Another barrier that keeps people feeling stuck and choosing to withhold apologies is feeling "justified". Feeling justified is connected to believing you are justified. If you believe you were hurt first or more deeply than the other person, you may believe that your actions are justified and that the other party should apologize first or does not even deserve an apology. At the end of the day, arguments like these manifest a disposition, an "attitude" that demands, "You go first!" or "I have nothing to apologize for!" Riding the waves of these kinds of emotions and beliefs is terribly unproductive. If both people are thinking the same thing, you can imagine how futile, hurtful and even devastating this can be to any relationship.

Regardless of whether or not you are able to prove you were hurt first, there is no way to prove who was hurt more! Seeing this kind of attitude at work in the wounded relationships of many couples and families has taught me that you can be right about an issue yet place yourself in the wrong because of your attitude. Choosing to adopt an attitude that refuses to acknowledge the other's pain renders one guilty of willfully inflicting pain on someone they profess to care for. Not only does this type of behavior qualify as cruel, but it also demonstrates a lack of maturity.

Oh, wow Drew, that's harsh and a little unrealistic. Are you suggesting that I just turn the other cheek? That I just forget that I too, have been wronged?! Now hold on, while I am in favour of extending forgiveness liberally, I am not encouraging you to automatically and summarily excuse the wrongs done to you. Taking that approach is not a healthy solution and can cause additional problems. No, what I am saying is, if you truly care about the person, seek to be the first to apologize. In fact, do it as quickly as possible. If you find yourself saying, "I have nothing to apologize for!" you are most likely wrong. In most significant relationships, heated arguments involve inaccurate assumptions, accusations, disrespectful tones and hurtful words.

As imperfect beings, there's usually some error that we can acknowledge and try to do differently in the future. As suggested before, you can make this a personal goal, race to apologize first. You may not always reach the finish line first, but in this case, a close second is still a win! Being the first to offer a Genuine Apology is a demonstration of maturity and an act of love that will help you to feel better, whether or not the person you apologize to is receptive.

I was asked the question, "What's the difference between apologizing first and compromising?" Compromising involves meeting the other person halfway, which sometimes means making concessions. While choosing to apologize first means laying aside your grievances for a moment, it does not always involve a mutual exchange or a balancing of the scales.

Being willing to seek the other person's healing ahead of your own may feel like a compromising of your "position", however, I believe it is an intentional shift in focus that allows you to adjust your priorities. When this shift occurs, it is no longer about who is right or who is wrong, who will win or who will lose. Even though you are no longer focusing on winning an argument or attempting to balance the scales, when you open the door to accepting responsibility for your actions, other people no longer feel blamed or attacked which puts you back on the same team.

As a secondary benefit, when we put the healing of others first in a genuine way there will most likely be room and support to address our needs next. Whether or not it happens right away, a Genuine Apology is usually followed by acceptance, forgiveness and an apology in return. That was the case for the father I spoke of earlier. Despite years of painful arguments and repeated seasons of toll-taking silence, this father's willingness to learn and use the art of a Genuine Apology not only helped him to reconnect with his daughter, but granted him the apology his heart longed for but his voice would never express. Her immediate offering of a heartfelt apology in return is something he, nor I, were expecting, nor will we ever forget. Watching their hurts and misunderstandings get washed away with Genuine Apologies was such an honour.

You see, it is possible to move beyond the fear of unpleasant emotions and the cold, hardened "You go first" or "You don't deserve an apology" attitude into the warmth of humility and forgiveness by offering a Genuine Apology. So, try not to let old patterns of fear, pride, insecurity or unhelpful attitudes get in the way of what means the most to you.

Family Patterns

Speaking of patterns, most of the early learning in our families stem from patterns that have been in play for generations. Generational patterns can have a remarkable and lasting impact on us as individuals throughout our entire lives. Although unseen, the direct or indirect messages and practices around apologies has had a significant impact on us and our relationships.

The patterns we experience as children help to inform the culture and rules around offering apologies that can stay with us forever. Past experiences of apologies are the building blocks from which we construct many of the problematic beliefs and attitudes noted earlier that inform how we view and approach apologies in our adult lives.

How many of you have heard phrases like, "Men don't apologize", "People will take advantage of you" or "people will think you are weak if you are always saying sorry." Believe it or not, all of these are examples of explicit beliefs and direct messages learned in families.

Some people grew up in homes where apologies were explicitly discouraged while in other families the messages were more subtle and indirect, solidified over time into implicit family patterns and rules that dictate what behaviors are appropriate around offering apologies. Consider if you will, someone who has never heard or witnessed an apology in their home. Believe it or not, it does happen. Having never seen or experienced apologies, such an individual could conclude that exchanging apologies is not something family members do with each other.

What of someone who has seen people apologize but continue to exhibit the same behavior again and again? They may have internalized the following phrase,

"Apologies don't mean anything!" Such experiences and conclusive statements can cultivate the belief that the act of apologizing is not necessary and emboss the expectation that people will, or should, just "get over it". Can you see the pattern that would emerge?

Such beliefs can be born from situations ranging from broken promises to all kinds of abuse. Am I being over-dramatic? I don't think so. The fact is, an observed behavior can lead to a conclusion, which becomes a belief, which then becomes the basis for other beliefs that dictate our behaviors and form family patterns. This process of witnessing, concluding, believing and acting on our beliefs is what happens in every family and is then passed on from one generation to the next. If this was your experience, then taking a look at how apologies, or the lack of apologies, informed your early years can be the key to engaging in Genuine Apologies and bringing healing to your most significant relationships. I have included a few examples of questions we would consider at an Art of a Genuine Apology Workshop.

For your consideration

Addressing Family Patterns

If you realize you have difficulty apologizing and

are wondering if it has anything to do with your childhood experiences, you can ask yourself the following questions:

1) What was I taught explicitly and/or implicitly about saying sorry?

2) Try to recall situations that would have warranted an apology and try to recall whether or not one was given. If so, what did it look, sound and feel like? If not, what prevented the apology/apologies from being offered?

3) If you can recall inadequate or hurtful apologies or interactions, what would you have liked to experience instead?

If after answering the questions above you continue to find it hard to apologize, I urge you to consider how you want to be treated when you've been wronged and compare that to how you treat others when you've hurt them. Having a clear picture of how you want to treat others will help you to carry it out. Whether you're a parent, spouse or a very close friend, remember that your choices are having an impact on individuals, who impact families and communities for generations to come. Your level of awareness and intentionality matters and can make a big difference.

Although I mentioned this earlier, it bears repeating here. When faced with challenging situations, it is important to critically examine our own thoughts and beliefs in order to assess the appropriateness of our emotional responses and reactions. Once again, our ability to manage our emotions points to our level of maturity.

The ability to critically examine our psychological responses and determine how to act in light of them, or even despite them, is also a sign of emotional maturity. Managing our emotions well means we will not try to avoid, dismiss or, worst of all, be lead and controlled by them. An emotionally mature person will seek to respond intentionally versus react emotionally. As you might guess, emotional maturity - the ability to be response-able directly informs your ability to master the art of a Genuine Apology.

This ability to respond, to manage one's emotions and to master the art of a Genuine Apology is only developed with attention, time and practice. Sometimes formal support is also helpful. The remaining chapters will show you what that support might look like and how the art of a Genuine Apology can begin to be developed.

Bringing A Genuine Apology to Life

Welcome to the next phase of learning the art of a Genuine Apology. By way of review, the first phase and portion of the book was all about the nuts and bolts of varying levels of apologies which led to the second segment, understanding what a Genuine Apology is composed of, what sets it apart from all other apologies and how it bridges forgiveness and reconciliation together to bring about healing in our most significant relationships. We then began to further prepare you for the journey by highlighting the things that could spoil your attempts as well as beliefs that can be barriers to giving or receiving a Genuine Apology. Now we enter the third and final phase, where we will observe the assembling of all the parts and pieces and learn about the packaging and delivery of a Genuine Apology.

To pull it all together and see how a Genuine Apology works, we will look at a situation where an apology was not only warranted but necessary for a couple to recover and rebuild their relationship.

 The Not So Perfect Family

After being employed by what seemed like a stable company for the past 25 years, Jonathan was let go as the company he worked for "right-sized". Even though they provided a severance package, it was clearly not enough to continue to support his wife, Maggie (a committed mother who did not return to work after their first child was born 18 years ago) and their 4 children, the eldest of whom was entering his first year of University. Jonathan prided himself on being the provider for his family and practically had a heart attack when his source of income and security was snatched away from him. In that moment, he perceived his family to be at great risk and blamed himself for not being prepared for this turn of events.

Feeling panicked and unsure of what to do, Jonathan decided to figure out what his options were before breaking the news to Maggie and the kids. One day turned into a week, that week turned into a month, then three and four.

Monday to Friday, Jonathan got dressed for work just as he always did, so that his family life would not be disrupted. While he maintained certain parts of his routine, everything else had changed. He interacted less frequently with Maggie and the kids for fear of them discovering that he had been let go. As the days passed, he grew more and more distant from them. His family was the biggest part of his sense of joy and purpose and without connecting with them he began to sink into a depression.

This depression came on slowly, so slowly that he didn't realize it was happening. To make matters worse, after each long day of job searching, he was irritable and short with the people he loved the most and found relief in a beer or two or three or ... I'm sure you get the picture. He couldn't offer an explanation for his mood and watched his own bitterness and resentment grow as his family members continued to live full lives around him, laughing, spending, having a grand old time, without knowing, without noticing what was happening to him.

It wasn't like this every day, there were moments of laughter and relief for Jonathan too, but the depressing waves of life soon returned, ripping his family, his foundation, from under his feet, overwhelming him with debt, fear, anger and hopelessness. The good times became fewer and fewer and the times between them became longer and longer. There were several interviews that revived his hopes for recovering all he had lost, but each rejection pulled him deeper.

Despite his best efforts, seven months into a relentless job search, Jonathan continued to come up empty. He even reconnected with old colleagues and friends in hopes of someone knowing of an opportunity that would help him and his family. Cynthia, was one of his old friends from University, who happened to be the head of Human Resources at a well-established company. She committed to keeping his resume at the top of the pile, however, even they were experiencing a hiring freeze.

Jonathan called Cynthia, as well as other contacts, on a weekly basis desperate for any available opportunity. During one of these calls to Cynthia, Jonathan's pride crumbled and his 7 months of silence broke. He began to talk about his decision to protect his family from the stress he was enduring, and about how exhausted he was. Cynthia offered sincere support and a listening ear for Jonathan, which became a relief from the secrecy and loneliness that was swallowing him alive.

13 months had passed and Jonathan's savings, the family's savings, were entirely depleted. It was at his lowest point when Jonathan received a call for a second interview for a position that could answer his prayers. He called Cynthia. Naturally, she expressed excitement

and offered whatever support she could. He went for the interview, dazzled the panel of interviewers and was offered the job! Right away, he called Cynthia. Instead of going home, he celebrated with Cynthia. It was in a picturesque moment, over a glass of wine and a wonderful meal at a quaint restaurant that he realized his feelings for her had grown beyond friendship. It was also in that moment that the notorious neighborhood gossip, Gloria, sent his wife a text about how well Jonathan looked at this restaurant and commented on how trusting she was to allow her husband to go to dinner with such an attractive woman, without her.

After Jonathan and Cynthia finished their meal and got up to leave, Jonathan saw Gloria, the ever-watchful neighbor who waved cordially announcing the crumbling wall of secrecy between him, his wife and their four children, that had stood impenetrable for the last 13 months.

When Jonathan arrived home, feeling confused, guilty, ashamed, fearful and heartbroken, he expected to be confronted by an angry and hurt wife, accusing him of having an affair. Instead, the house was silent. The kids were out and when he called for Maggie, there was no answer. After searching the upstairs rooms, he began to fear the worst, he raced to the last place he had not checked, his office in the basement where he found her in front of his computer, tears running down her face as she for the first time, in more than 20 years of their relationship, doubted his faithfulness. She sat paralyzed in his chair after having read through many emails that featured numerous endearing exchanges between him and Cynthia as well as bank statements that revealed the devastating reality of their financial situation. She had no words for Jonathan that night, the next day or the three weeks that followed.

Jonathan's previously depressing silence was met with an even greater silence. Despite starting a new job and being clear with Cynthia that he had no intentions to move beyond "friendship" and had made a mistake by having dinner with her that night, Jonathan's greatest fear of his family falling apart was actually materializing.

One ordinary Monday, three weeks into his new job, Maggie broke her silence. Without making eye contact, in a soft, hesitant, yet determined voice she asked, "Jon... what did you do?" Relieved yet ashamed and broken, Jonathan fell to his knees, wrapped his arms tightly around her waist and wept. Between heaving and sobbing, his normally rich and weighty baritone voice whispered and crackled the words, "I am so sorry, Honey. I am so so sorry".

Despite many conversations, explanations and

sincere apologies, it didn't seem to take. Jonathan and Maggie struggled to rebuild trust and move past the hurt but all they could do was fight. Maggie was now experiencing bouts of anxiety and depression that were only interrupted by flashes of anger and accusations of Jonathan's unfaithfulness. At first, Jonathan accepted Maggie's outbursts and periods of withdrawal, however, three months later his patience, understanding and even his guilt gave way to anger.

The breaking point that brought this couple to my office, was the day their 11-year-old daughter, Leyla, accidentally left her diary open on her bed. Maggie, fell to pieces when she read about Leyla wanting to die because she believed her parents were going to get a divorce. Maggie called Jonathan at work and demanded that they go for counselling right away.

Even though Leyla didn't have a clear picture of where it all began or what was happening between her parents, the experience of this family tells the common story of the transmission of anxiety, hurt and depression from one member of the family to the others. Thankfully, Jonathan and Maggie's commitment to the welfare of their children enabled them to come together and get some help.

After hearing the details of their story, it was

clear that Maggie and Jonathan wanted to repair their relationship but didn't know how. They acknowledged that apologies were offered over and over again, yet they struggled to overcome the barriers of deep hurt and resentment. Because fights tended to erupt when apologies were offered, they began to see apologizing as counterproductive. Together, we examined their cycles of conflict, particularly their recent attempts at apologizing. They noted many of the apology spoilers you read about earlier, including 'buts' and explanations and described body language that incited further anger.

While the details of Maggie and Jonathan's experience differ from other relationships, much of their experiences around apologies are similar to countless apologies run amok. I find it painful to think of the many relationships that are further damaged by unhelpful apologies, apologies that are demanded or offered incessantly and worst of all, apologies that are short lived. I have learned that the cure to these experiences are both woven into a Genuine Apology and birthed out of a Genuine Apology.

After reviewing their apologies and noting the things to avoid I walked them through the four steps that spell the word LIVE when offering a Genuine Apology. Maggie and Jonathan were instantly able to see where they were going wrong in their past attempts and wanted to use the steps right then and there. Jonathan volunteered to go first. Just as you are about to see, Jonathan and Maggie learned how each step emphasized one or more of the values we discussed earlier but the best part of a Genuine Apology is that it intentionally positioned them to live out their apology after it was offered. In the chapters that follow, I will walk you through each step of Jonathan's experience of building and offering a Genuine Apology so that you have a chance to observe what he did well and the challenges he experienced along the way.

Step 1
List and Label

Before sharing how Jonathan offered his Genuine Apology I will outline the first step. The building of a Genuine Apology begins by listing and labeling the specific actions you want to apologize for. This is not an easy task for most people. Humility is definitely required to move in this direction. Taking this initial step also allows the value of responsibility to be seen and clearly heard by the person you are apologizing to. I encourage people to literally make a list of the actions, decisions or behaviors they want to apologize for before offering an apology. I will share more about why this is so helpful a little later, but for now, just know that being specific about the actions you are sorry for is an important step in helping others know that you are sincere and have actually given thought to what you are saying.

Jonathan was ready to offer his apology. Although he didn't have a list in front of him, he had rehearsed the sequence of events for months and was well prepared to take ownership for his actions. The first thing Jonathan did was turn and face Maggie. He was off to a great start! Looking directly into her eyes, he said, "Hun, I am so sorry for all of the things I put you through this past year, but you have to know that I didn't intend to hurt you or the kids."

His sincerity was communicated well by his body language and she was reciprocating right up until she heard the 'but'. After that, she instantly tensed up and the softness in her eyes was replaced with a cold glare. Another apology spoiled with a 'but'! And that wasn't the only issue at hand, he was telling her what she "had to know" and believe. Although that's clearly what he wanted and probably what she wanted too, telling her what she had to do was a wrong move! I jumped in and reminded Jonathan to leave out the 'buts' at all costs and brought to his attention the fact that he was telling her what she *had* to believe. He had no idea that this was how he was coming across and apologized.

Surprisingly, Maggie smiled and commented, "You're apologizing about your apology. I can't tell if you're really good or really bad at this."

Although Jonathan was a little embarrassed, he laughed and acknowledged feeling totally incompetent.

I reminded him of the fact that most of us were not taught how to apologize well. This was also the perfect opportunity to point out the fact that beyond sincerity and correctly focused intentions, the first step to offering a Genuine Apology is being specific about what you'd like to apologize for. I asked him to identify the first thing he'd like to apologize for and to be very specific about what it was because this is the first place most apologies fall short.

Just as I mentioned to him, I want to convey to you, that when offering an apology, it is critical that you label the specific behavior, action or choice that you believe had a negative impact on the other person. Remember, simply saying, "I am sorry", no matter how sincere you are, is simply inadequate. And, a general apology that attempts to cover all of the hurts someone has experienced is usually only well received if you're dying. Outside of that, it's best to begin with one instance and move on to the next and the next and the next.

Jonathan appreciated the advice and made a second attempt. "I don't know where to begin. This started so long ago... Maggie, I want to apologize for not telling you when I lost my job, I was just so angry and embarrassed..." I interrupted just in time to save this apology from ruin as he was about to start sharing the reasons for his choices.

"Jonathan, I appreciate that you want Maggie to understand what contributed to you not telling her that you lost your job, however, it is important that your apology doesn't turn into an appeal for sympathy or an explanation of your actions. This apology is about acknowledging how your decisions have impacted Maggie."

"Wow, you're right Drew, I didn't realize I was doing that... this is hard."

"What exactly is making this so hard?" I asked, to which Jonathan replied,

"I really want Maggie to understand how this happened. Won't she feel better if she understands that I didn't mean for this happen?" I looked to Maggie who was trying very hard to stay silent.

"Jon, I know you didn't mean for any of this to happen, but that doesn't change the fact that it did happen."

"Jonathan," I soberly interjected, "that's why this first step is so important. It strictly acknowledges the facts and demonstrates you are taking responsibility despite the good intentions that led you down this road. And, furthermore, any explanation you offer is most likely going to sound like an excuse." Jonathan took a deep breath and made another attempt.

"Maggie, I want to apologize for not telling you the day that I was let go or at least the day after the shock had worn off." Let's pause here and discuss what we've seen so far.

It took some time for Jonathan to make his way through step 1. Although this step sounds simple enough, you can see there are a number of things to tend to as well as potential barriers to overcome at the same time. There is no doubt in my mind that Jonathan was sincere, but it may have been tough for him to muster up the courage to attempt to apologize once again, especially with a third party in the room. Nevertheless, he took the plunge, moved past feeling awkward and honed in on ensuring that Maggie was the focal point of his attention. His body language made this unquestionable. This first step can be quite difficult but Jonathan did an amazing job by being humble, putting aside his feelings, remaining open to guidance and very specific about what he was apologizing for.

As stated earlier, being specific about what you are apologizing for can help the person you're apologizing to, but I also want to highlight how it can help you, particularly if you have mixed emotions. The truth is, despite feeling guilty for the many unwise decisions he made, Jonathan was also feeling unappreciated and angry as he thought about the unacknowledged silent suffering he endured while he attempted to keep his family protected from the fear and anxiety of not having an income. Remember, he bore this weight alone for 7 months without telling a soul. Jonathan's anger and hurt could have allowed him to feel justified or think that he was being demeaned by being the only one to apologize. These thoughts could have lead him to believe that the situation was unfair. Jonathan avoided being dragged away from a Genuine Apology by staying focused on taking responsibility for very specific actions.

Taking responsibility is the exact opposite of what happens in the most hurtful apologies. Can you imagine where this conversation would have gone if Jonathan said, "I'm sorry. Keeping this secret from you and sharing it with Cynthia was a mistake." That would be a mistake alright! Almost as big a mistake as going to dinner with Cynthia without Maggie knowing in the first place. Even though both of these decisions are errors in judgment, using the word mistake somehow oversimplifies the decision-making process. While it may be hard to be honest and accept responsibility, if you love and care for the person you have hurt, your love will find its best expression if you put their needs before yours, be humble enough to take full responsibility for your actions when you apologize.

The reality is, many people have a hard time being humble, acknowledging their errors and accepting responsibility. If this description sounds like you, consider this a gentle wake up call. You might not know it, but your inability to offer a Genuine Apology can be extremely hurtful to those you care about. This kind of hurt often moves people to try to force others to accept responsibility and apologize. If you are being forced to apologize, I encourage you to think about whether or not you have a hard time with humbly acknowledging where you've gone wrong.

If, on the other hand, you find yourself trying to force others to apologize, give it up and let it go. You will do more harm than good. I have learned that forcing someone to accept responsibility or to apologize doesn't work well in intimate relationships. If someone is unwilling to accept responsibility, don't waste your time trying to convince or force them to. Thankfully, Jonathan was ready and willing to apologize, however, if he was caught behind one of the many barriers to offering a Genuine Apology and Maggie tried to force him to apologize, he might have complied but would it have been sincere and meaning-full? Probably not. She might think she is holding him accountable, however, accountability in a loving relationship is something that must be desired and willfully accepted.

Most people don't realize this, but demanding an apology from someone often moves that person further away from acknowledging where they went wrong. The moment someone is forced to "take responsibility" the interaction suddenly turns into enforcement which is controlling and experienced as punishment. That's not what relationships are about, that's what police and prisons are for. Living out that dynamic in a relationship is not something that anyone I know would sign up for. In my experience, forcing someone to apologize doesn't yield the kind of apology that breathes life into relationships. Even if an apology is given under such circumstances, it is likely to be insincere, which will be satisfying if we are only concerned about winning. If that is the case, then you were likely not looking for a Genuine Apology and would benefit from looking beyond the hurtful situation and figuring out what you're really in search of.

Although apologizing sounds simple, I hope by now we can agree that it is not always easy. The fact that one can come across barriers to taking the very first step in offering a Genuine Apology is reason enough for this book to be written. If you're struggling with listing and labeling the actions, decisions or choices that you believe have had a negative impact on someone you care about, take a look at some of the following tips.

For your consideration

How Helpful Is Listing And Labeling Your Actions?

When I am hesitant about doing something, I turn my attention to the positive outcome that awaits me. As noted above, the person you are apologizing to will see that you actually took the time to recall the incident but are also seeing you take responsibility. I think it is obvious how this will be helpful to the other person and in addition to helping you move past possible mixed emotions as described in Jonathan's situation, there are a few more things it can do for you. Even though you may never show them your list, taking responsibility goes a long way towards improving their impression of you and your reputation. There is nothing wrong with accepting that we are imperfect beings who will go wrong from time to time, however, no one wants to be around someone who refuses to take responsibility for their actions. Your list will help you be a more desirable person.

Another benefit of listing and labeling your actions is that this step invites you to recall the event and to focus on what you want to apologize for. Many couples remember sequences of events and details very differently which makes it easy to get caught up in trying to sort out who is right or wrong. Our bird's eye-view of Jonathan's story helped us to appreciate that there are many single incidents that are a part of a larger story; too many to spend time trying to agree upon.

Instead of spending the time and energy trying to figure out or agree on details and timelines, you can simplify the process and take responsibility for your part, regardless of where or how it started. Making a list and labeling our actions helps us to focus on what we have done wrong, which most people don't argue about. Although we are focusing on our own actions, step 1 helps us to take a step back and be as objective as possible which not only allows you to identify actions you're not proud of but can help you see the larger picture more clearly as well.

Seeing the big picture of your relationship is more beneficial when approaching an apology than you might think. Too many people waste time blaming the other person. I have never seen blaming actually help a situation. The cure for blaming someone is taking responsibility for your actions which can inspire and allow them to take responsibility for theirs in the current situation as well as in future situations. Can you see the larger picture? As alluded to above, very rarely will someone stop you from taking responsibility for hurting them. When you focus on taking responsibility as opposed to blaming, the risk of arguing over the details decreases significantly making this and the conversations that follow much easier to have. Although taking responsibility can be tough, it can make the rest of your life much better.

If you find yourself stuck behind the "You hurt me too!" barrier, taking this first step can really help you break through it. Yes, you may be hurt because of what someone has said or how they approached you about an issue, but that doesn't change the facts about the things you are responsible for, nor does it close the door on your opportunity to take responsibility for your part. Simply address the decisions you made that you are not proud of. If we are honest and committed to personal growth, there will always be things we can identify as areas for improvement. Focus on finding those things and letting the people you care about know that you are not satisfied or happy with the choice(s) that you've made. In most cases, by addressing your part and offering a Genuine Apology, you will have more success at conveying your concerns about their inappropriate or hurtful actions when the appropriate time arrives.

Words May Say It, But Body Language Displays It

Although it may be hard, ensuring that you make eye contact and that your tone of voice and body language matches the sentiment you want to convey is critical. When your body language matches the words and your sentiment, then your communication is congruent. If your body language is off, you can unintentionally communicate many things including disinterest or a lack of gravity and disaster will follow within seconds. Some examples of body language that can communicate disinterest or a lack of gravity include not directly facing the person you're apologizing to, refusing to make eye contact and engaging in something else like texting, paying bills or doing laundry.

It sounds odd, but we humans do strange things when we feel unpleasant emotions. Although the tone of your voice may convey humility it alone may not be enough to help the person see that you are seriously attempting to take responsibility. Taking responsibility for your actions really means a lot to other people so be sure that your body language doesn't cause you to look insincere. Incongruent body language can convey the exact opposite of what you are trying to say. Remember, body language and other forms of nonverbal communication can totally transform your message, so be aware and intentional as you take this first step.

How To Help Others Take Responsibility

As difficult as taking responsibility for one's actions is, I think waiting for others to do the same is even harder. I've already noted that forcing others to apologize does not improve the health of one's relationship but I want to mention some things that you can do when someone is struggling to take responsibility or appears to be nowhere close to apologizing. For starters, whether we are interacting with a spouse, partner, family member or friend, we are always modeling how well or how poorly things can be done. Your first role or opportunity to impact change is to be an inspiring example.

I briefly mentioned it earlier, but allow me to say it more clearly, being aware that our actions can inspire others is invaluable. Our ability to inspire others is far more powerful than our attempts to control them. You can teach people how to accept responsibility and apologize well by modeling it. People learn more from what we do than what we say, so look for opportunities to practice offering a Genuine Apology. I am sure that there will be many opportunities for us all, for the rest of our lives.

Another way to impact change and encourage someone to take responsibility is to help them modify their language or use more accurate words. If someone attempts to apologize using the words 'accident' or 'mistake', be sure to assess how true this is. If there was willful action involved and simply a lack of forethought or consideration, don't let that stop you from stating what the truth of the situation is. Be sure to ask them if they actually considered how their choices would hurt you or not. Asking a question like this invites people to reflect on their choices and gives them the opportunity to be more honest with you.

From reading this chapter, you can see how the art of a Genuine Apology promotes being proficient at recognizing and taking responsibility. The more comfortable you are with taking responsibility is the more comfortable you'll be at gracefully helping others to do the same. After years of practice, it's pretty easy for me to point out where others have gone wrong. Although it sounds funny, it's also very true. If you're not accustomed to asking direct questions, this process may be very uncomfortable. It may even feel like an interrogation. Just remember, giving someone the opportunity to acknowledge whether or not they gave thought to their actions is a lot kinder than simply accusing them and writing them off.

If you're afraid to have these kinds of interactions

you may be tempted to turn a blind eye to the situation. Unfortunately, people who routinely try to avoid accepting responsibility are enabled by those who routinely sweep things under the rug. You might not know it, but you can become the escape this person uses to avoid accepting responsibility. If you want to help this person grow and remove yourself from this kind of interaction, refuse to let her/him off the hook!

Just as I mentioned in chapter 4, some people believe that in order to forgive you have to forget. That is not true! Forgetting and forgiving are not synonymous. You can acknowledge the facts and forgive at the same time. Helping others acknowledge this fact can do more than change avoidance or denial into an apology, it can change the course of your relationship and the other person's life!

What To Do While You Wait For A Genuine Apology

A Genuine Apology is life changing, so waiting for one can feel torturous. For those of you who have been waiting far too long for a Genuine Apology, it might seem that you are destined to remain hurt until you receive the apology you desire, but that is not necessarily true. There are a couple of things you can do if someone you care about seems to be having trouble taking the first step at offering a Genuine Apology.

First, you can give some thought to what makes it hard for the other person to apologize. Then when the time is right, you can share your observations and theories and ask them if you're perceiving it accurately. A statement like this might be useful, "I am wondering if part of the reason for your choosing not to apologize is that you think I am just as responsible for the situation as you are." If they agree then you have the opportunity to acknowledge your part and model how it's done. Sometimes being wrong about a theory can be a good thing. Many times people appreciate this approach so much (as opposed to being told what their problem is) that they open up about what is really making it difficult. Then you get to ask them to help you understand more about it and how that came to be.

Please be aware that considering the theories and logical explanations for their behavior before speaking with them is not about "getting it right". For you to be successful with this strategy, it is important to have the goal of cultivating compassion in your mind and heart so that you can be helpful if they choose to be vulnerable about what makes apologizing difficult for them. At the heart of this strategy is a desire for increased vulnerability, intimacy and ongoing communication.

Another strategy to use when Genuine Apologies

are hard to come by, is simply letting the person know how you feel about the situation and that you want them to be aware of the impact their actions have had on you. While this conversation may only feature your acknowledgement of the impact you will likely feel better about the situation and be able to move on even without an apology simply because it was acknowledged in their hearing. However, if you believe it is important for the words "I'm sorry" to accompany the acknowledgement, you are likely to receive what you hope for if you let the person know that their offering of an apology would mean a lot to you if or when he or she means it. Then, you wait. It is important for you to remember that if the person doesn't believe they are at fault or wrong, it may never happen. So, give adequate thought about what is really important to you and why that it the case.

Define What You Really Want

When feeling hurt, many people desire an explanation or at least an acknowledgment of the wrong done to them. These desires are virtually automatic, but it is important to be clear about what you really want in these scenarios. If you just want to hear the words, "I'm sorry" in order to move on with your life then I would argue that you are not looking for reconciliation and don't really desire a Genuine Apology. Terrible hurts and injustice can break loving bonds in significant relationships, leaving you feeling robbed and violated. In moments like these, people want to punish others or regain power by forcing them to apologize. If you've endured this kind of pain, be sure to take the time and space you need to figure out what will truly bring about your healing. Chances are, "I'm sorry" won't cut it.

In the most hurtful situations, many people find it hard to accept the reality of what has happened to them. They question themselves and discount their ability to validate the hurt they've experienced. Automatically blending your search for validation and acknowledgment with an apology and reconciliation can leave you vulnerable in a couple of ways. Although seeking validation and acknowledgment is only natural, expecting the person who hurt you to accept responsibility and acknowledge how they've impacted you is only realistic if you're dealing with a loving and mature person. If the person lacks these traits, then you are likely to be disappointed.

Too many people end up relentlessly following the lives of people who've hurt them, cyber-stalking them as if there is an unbreakable connection between their own perspective and the other person's acknowledgment of their experience. This is not the case! You are an individual. Believe that your perspective matters even when it is different than the perspectives of others.

This reality is closely related to one of the most maturing lessons I have learned from working through issues with families, including addressing my own family history: we put ourselves in a very vulnerable position when we pursue someone in hopes of receiving something from them that they didn't experience, and subsequently, don't possess. Expecting a Genuine Apology from someone who may never have witnessed or experienced one will almost certainly leave us disappointed.

Here's another dynamic that often leaves me perplexed. Perhaps it's our relational nature that contributes to us thinking if the other person is not sorry, then on some level we are deserving of their ill treatment of us or that something is wrong with us. We then end up looking for love from the people who have hurt us and believe that our healing is attached to their apology. This too, is not true! Convincing yourself to stay in a relationship for the purpose of accessing healing is not the solution. If you've been hurt by someone who appears to be indifferent or calloused to your pain, especially if you're not married to the person, don't wait for them to apologize, it may never happen. And, if it does, it may not be sincere. More importantly, whether you are married or not, you don't really need an apology from someone who doesn't care enough to help with the healing process. Don't allow those who don't actively care about you to hold you hostage by waiting for an apology. You can seek healing through prayer, forgiveness and the safety and presence of those who demonstrate maturity and love.

I will end this chapter with two important questions:

1. Who do you want to share a Genuine Apology with?

2. Are you ready to take the first step? If so, remember to make your list and keep in mind that you're not thinking generally about the relationship so that each situation or hurtful moment will have a list of its own.

Once you've answered those questions, we can move on to the second step.

Step 2
Imagine the Impact

One of my least favorite things in this world is traffic. That's putting it mildly. In fact, I hate traffic, especially when there seems to be no reason for it! I feel particularly frustrated by rubberneck drivers - drivers who slow down to get a good look at what is happening with other drivers. I agree that slowing down and giving space to Police Officers is important, however, the only thing that moves me away from my frustration with traffic is seeing a terrible accident. Immediately, I am no longer angry about the traffic and my heart and prayers are extended.

Although I try very hard not to, sometimes I become a rubberneck driver myself. Even though I wasn't in the accident, somehow, I am touched by their situation and am able to move beyond the unpleasant feelings associated with my own situation. Seeing the damage done to cars, streets signs and light posts automatically moves me to consider the physical impact of the accident on those things and more tragically, the impact on the people in the accident. When I begin to think about these things and feel shock, fear, concern, sympathy or sadness, I am experiencing empathy and that is what step 2 is all about.

The second step in offering a Genuine Apology is to imagine and express how your actions might have impacted the other person. Sadly, this critical step in offering a Genuine Apology is one that most people don't stop and consider. How can you offer a Genuine Apology if you don't take the time to think about how the other person was impacted by your actions? You simply can't. When you place yourself in the offended person's shoes and draw upon your ability to identify with the emotions the other person might be feeling, then and only then can you truly experience and express empathy.

I am keenly aware of the fact that "placing yourself in another person's shoes" is much easier said than done. The first challenge that most people have with this task is being able to shift their focus from their own experience to someone else's. In the case of a terrible accident, it is a little easier, because the impact is pretty obvious and we are often shocked right out of focusing on our own situations. It's also a little easier in such drastic scenarios because most people will likely agree about how serious an accident is. When we see a car that appears to have flipped over many times before rolling into a ditch and catching on fire, we start to wonder, *"Could they have made it out alive?"* However, if we see a minor fender bender in the middle lane of the expressway, we might probably think to ourselves, *What's wrong with you! That's not a big deal... urhhh, get out of the way... move over to the shoulder!!!!!!* Assessing or evaluating scenarios is an automatic and even a healthy way to function. Unfortunately, our automatic assessing of situations applies to emotionally damaging situations just as much. If we're honest, because we can't see another person's pain, we tend to take the same attitude as we would about a seemingly minor car accident, and wonder, *What is the big deal? Get over it already!*

If you haven't noticed, the automatic assessment moved from being an analytical evaluation to judgmental criticism where we assume we know what others are thinking and feeling, dictate what they should be thinking and feeling and then engage in thinking and feeling negatively about them. At this point we are well off course. Even if we are successful at getting back on track and shifting our focus to the other person's experience it will be even more important to try to see things from their perspective. If we evaluate the situation and form a judgment about the other person based on how we see things or how we intended to do things, we will miss out on imagining the different ways the other person could be seeing and experiencing the same situation.

I know this might be a little confusing, but bear with me just a moment longer. In order to keep myself from experiencing road rage I play a little game that involves imagining different scenarios that offer acceptable reasons for the "ridiculous" choices other drivers make. Yes, I am aware that I form judgments about other drivers when I am frustrated, however, I have honed the skill of thinking of alternatives which helps me to let go of the original storyline in my mind that would otherwise keep me frustrated. So, in the case of someone driving in the far-left lane on the expressway, going twenty kilometres (or worse yet, miles) beneath the speed limit, I have imagined that this person's vehicle is somehow unable to get up to the speed limit and the driver, who is a faithful hardworking parent just trying to get home, is trying to stay close to the shoulder and doesn't realize that the hazard lights are not on.

This picture enables me to move past my initial feelings of frustration and allows me to calmly change lanes and go about my merry way. You might be saying, "Andrew, that's not really the case..." You might be right. I don't know if the picture I am painting in my head is accurate and because I am not trying to apologize to this person, that is not my objective. I am simply highlighting a way to practice seeing things from a different perspective. As it relates to offering a Genuine Apology, it is best to acknowledge that you might not know how the other person feels. In fact, the only way to know with any degree of certainty is if the person has told you. Until they do, practicing this skill will help you to cultivate empathy.

Cultivating empathy is not to be confused with feeling sympathy and excusing immature or inappropriate behavior. The purpose of incorporating this skill into your Genuine Apology is to prevent you from being stuck seeing things solely from your point of view. This skill is difficult for many to exercise, but it is essential if you want to be able to truly connect on an emotional level with another person. If you are unable to imagine how the other person could see and experience the situation then you might be dismissive, think they are overreacting or tell yourself they are crazy. None of these judgmental options will help you to apologize well.

I also want to emphasize the benefits of staying away from concluding that you *know* how someone feels. When we express empathy, while acknowledging that we don't know what the other person is feeling, we can minimize the possibility of them feeling belittled, manipulated or controlled. Most people don't like to be told what to do and can feel just as irritated when they are told how they "must" feel. This is especially true when people are feeling upset or vulnerable, particularly with the person who may have contributed to them feeling the way they do.

As noted in earlier chapters, people may find it hard to tolerate their own emotions and may be very guarded in discussions about them. Even if you mean well, when you tell someone how they feel, it can be experienced as invasive and presumptive, which may cause them to take a defensive posture. Even though I am encouraging you to attempt to imagine how someone else is feeling and to acknowledge these feelings, I want to clearly note that you are not responsible to label their emotions accurately without their help because that would be the same as reading their minds, which is impossible.

Instead, you'll fare much better by hypothesizing. Yes, I am suggesting that you make an educated guess. Whether someone is uncomfortable with being vulnerable or doesn't want to engage with their own emotions, you are more likely to be able to move forward with your apology by acknowledging your beliefs about what they may be feeling in the form of a theory. After stating the behaviors that you believe have impacted the other person negatively, instead of saying, "You must hate me", you could say, "I imagine that you're feeling terribly angry" or "If I were you, I'd be feeling exhausted and discouraged." Expressing empathy in the form of a theory removes the possibility of you being accused of presuming to know someone *so* well while getting it *so* wrong!

Just in case the importance of this step isn't clear, I want to share the anticipated impact of including this step in your Genuine Apology. When we show true empathy by acknowledging how someone might be feeling or might have felt, it begins to impact their emotional experience and can shift their perspective of you and the relationship in an instant. When this step is executed well, the other person feels valued, heard and connected to you. You can usually tell if what you've imagined is accurate because the person tends to give you their undivided attention, makes eye contact, nods their head and may even say that you're right.

Now that we know how this step works, let's go back to step 1 of Jonathan's Genuine Apology and walk through the development of step 2.

Jonathan took a deep breath and made another attempt. *(Step 1)* "Maggie, I want to apologize for not telling you the day that I was let go, or at least the day after the shock had worn off.

(Step 2) "I will never forget the day I found you in front of the computer, crying. You looked stunned and heart-broken. If I were you I would have been so hurt, so betrayed and so angry. I imagine you felt all of those feelings and probably more." Maggie replied,

"Yes, I felt all of those emotions, eventually. But at first I didn't feel anything but shock..., Jonny, that day, you broke my heart. I know you didn't sleep with her, but I don't know if I will ever be able to trust you again." Before Jonathan could respond to Maggie's last words, I chose to intervene because I had a sense that he was about to do what most people do at this point, panic!

"I hate to interrupt at such a sensitive moment, yet it is important to realize this is also a critical moment. Jonathan, it looks as if you were about to attempt to convince Maggie that you've learned your lesson and that you can be trusted or ask her what you can do to prove it, but before you do, I want you to repeat what you heard Maggie say."

"She said, that she will never trust me again, but that can't be true..." I interrupted, as I am known to do,

"Actually, that's not what she said. It sounded to me like she said you were right about her feeling hurt and angry yet beyond that, her heart is broken and she doesn't know if she will be *able* to trust you again... her heart is broken... a broken heart needs to be mended before it can fully trust again." Jonathan turned to Maggie and said,

"I can see that your heart is broken... that I broke your heart when I broke your trust, but are you willing to try to trust me again?"

"Actually Jonathan," I injected, "the fact that she is here speaking with you right now says a great deal, but the ball is still in your court."

"Really?" Queried stunned Jonathan, "How so, Andrew?" Let's pause here for a moment.

Perhaps you experience the back and forth between me sharing this heart-rending story and my commentary to you as frustrating, but I hope you will hang in there. It's of vital importance that you understand how well Jonathan is doing and what he is managing to avoid. He did so many things correctly! After labeling his actions, Jonathan described what he saw, saying that he will never forget the day he walked in to see her in front of the computer, crying. With one sentence he did two critical things. Number one, he kept the focus on her by describing what he saw and how she might have felt. When offering a Genuine Apology it is imperative to stick with focusing on the other person's experience as much as humanly possible. Remember, even though you will benefit from the apology on a number of levels, this moment is primarily about seeking healing for the other person's pain.

Number two, Jonathan did not talk about his feelings. If Jonathan had started talking about how he felt seeing her cry it could be experienced as him seeking sympathy from her, which would likely be experienced as upsetting and even manipulative. As opposed to a self-focused recounting of events, keeping your attention on the other person's experience is the best thing to do.

Another self-focused route to take is self-depricating in an apology. While you may feel guilty and think of yourself as the scum of the earth, describing yourself in negative terms or telling the person that they must be thinking negatively about you can cause the other person to be confused and upset. Here they are experiencing an apology and suddenly they are accused of thinking badly about you. Unexpectedly, you are now in the seat of the offended or hurting party, before you've even completed your apology. While it may not be your intention, this course of action can also cause people to feel guilty. Feeling guilty when someone is apologizing to you can also cause you to feel manipulated. When the time comes for you to offer a Genuine Apology, just like Jonathan, stay focused on what you've witnessed the other person experience as a result of your actions.

After acknowledging what he saw, Jonathan went on to say what he would have felt if he were in her position followed by the very objective of this step, an acknowledgement of what she "might" have felt. Although he referenced himself, the focus was still directed towards Maggie. And notice, he phrased it in the form of a possibility. The only time he concluded or expressed knowing what she felt was after she told him. Until he heard it from her lips, it could only be his assumption or a theory. Never conclude what someone is feeling until they tell you!

Because we accept that we don't know for sure what someone else has experienced until they tell us, it is important to leave room for them to inform us. As you can see from Maggie and Jonathan's experience, an apology isn't always just one person speaking. Thinking, observing and listening to yourself as well as the other person is the dynamic and interactive reality of a Genuine Apology. Had Jonathan stopped Maggie and said, "Just let me finish before you interrupt" he would have missed out on her joining the conversation and guiding his apology to where it needed to go in order to effectively address her hurt. It's almost as if she were taking his hand

and placing it right where she was hurt and saying this is where I feel the pain. This brings us back to the value of humility. Unless you are humble enough to receive guidance about what someone needs, that person will not likely feel safe enough to tell you what they need from you. In light of the fact that the other person knows what they need better than you do, be prepared to get it wrong and to be corrected in the process.

Despite Jonathan's fear of Maggie choosing not to trust him again, his willingness to accept responsibility and his openness to Maggie (and I) helping him get it right leads us directly into step number 3, to which we will turn after a few thoughts for your consideration.

For your consideration

How To Avoid Concluding

As noted above, do your best to avoid presuming to know what someone is feeling or thinking until they tell you. If you have a tendency to tell people what they are feeling or become aware that you have done this in the middle of your Genuine Apology, there is no harm in acknowledging it and rephrasing your statement. "You know what, please allow me to try this again, I tend to presume what you "must" be feeling and that's not how I want to go about this. I am trying to do things differently." People tend to be very gracious when others are acknowledging both their errors as well as being in the midst of learning. Instead of phrases like, *You must have been so hurt* or *You had to have been thinking…* opt for statements like, *If I were you I…* or *I can only imagine how _____ you were feeling…* or *You seemed so _____ by what I did. Did I get that right?*

What To Do If You Imagine The Impact Incorrectly

When attempting to acquire a new skill, you are likely to experience bumps, bruises and complete failures along the way. Practicing empathy and weaving it into your Genuine Apology in the form of a theory can be very challenging. So, what do you do if you get it wrong? If the person's reaction seems to suggest that you are way off or have even slightly missed the mark, you can ask for their help to get it right. Statements like those can be helpful, "It looks like I am wrong about how you felt. Could you help me understand… how you feel is important to me…"

Yes, you will be opening the door to a smart remark, but that is one of the risks that attempting to heal the hurt in your most significant relationships involve. Remind yourself that you can handle it and that you're invested, or you wouldn't be offering a Genuine Apology in the first place. With that said, let's turn to the step that requires the most time and thought to develop.

Step 3
Verbalize your commitment to a plan of Action

Most decent apologies stop after step 1. I believe many people would be shocked and thrilled to receive an apology that made it to step 2. Even if someone was pleased with your apology making it to the second step, there is great danger in stopping your apology before taking the third. Far too frequently, people forget about the apologies they've made and repeat the troublesome behavior. Not only does this upset the person you've apologized to again, but it ruins your credibility.

Far worse than ruining your credibility is eroding your sense of personal efficacy and your ability to change. When this happens, most people become frustrated with themselves to the point of giving up and saying, "This is just who I am, accept it." It may sound like a disrespectful and dismissive message to others, but before that message of resistance to change is voiced aloud, the cry of resignation is declared within. If you've heard this cry or voiced this message before, I want you to know that even the most sincere and well-meaning people have found themselves making the same mistakes and decisions over and over again, but this is not reason enough to lose hope. Please, don't give up yet! More often than not, giving up and losing hope is due to people not knowing about step 3 - Verbalizing your commitment to a plan of action. In order to verbalize your plan of action, you must first create and commit to a realistic plan for change.

While this may sound very simple, it can actually be quite a complex endeavour. You see, committing to a realistic plan for change is so much more than making a promise to never repeat the offending action again. Many people make promises but very few are able to keep them. I want to help people keep their promises. That's why step 3 involves the following components: making reparation where possible (as soon as possible), creating a realistic plan and verbalizing your commitment to that plan. Let's look at making reparation as it relates to a Genuine Apology.

What is reparation? To put it simply, reparation is taking action and repairing the relationship by replacing the item(s) or offering compensation where appropriate.

I encourage people to do this as soon as possible. By acting quickly, you demonstrate the importance of the situation and begin to highlight the significance of the person. Please, please, please don't get me wrong, I am not encouraging you to go out and buy flowers or something of that sort. That's the opposite of what I am saying. Save buying a gift, sending roses or chocolate for guilt-free moments, when you simply want to appreciate someone and lift their mood for a day or two. Although reparation can take the form of a gift, it is essential that the gift be relevant to the offense committed. In the context of a Genuine Apology, a gift of reparation will be a logical offering that conveys a true recognition of what you've done. This kind of gift will move you beyond the acknowledgment of guilt and will demonstrate remorse much more effectively than chocolate.

Even though it may seem trivial, a common issue that damages relationships between siblings will help to illustrate how reparation works. Many sisters (and brothers too) end up in conflict over clothing. If you've borrowed an article of clothing, especially without permission, and it was ruined or damaged, it makes logical and moral sense to replace it. If you cannot afford to replace it, perhaps you can save towards it and repay it as quickly as possible. Simply saying, "I'm sorry for taking and ruining your sweater" is insufficient even if your apology is sincere.

Words count, however, a Genuine Apology requires actions that are in keeping with the apology. Why should someone believe you're sorry if you willfully acted in a way that you knew would or could upset them. In cases like these, reparation is essential! When it comes to situations that are as clear-cut as borrowing clothes, asking the person for direction in respect to reparation can help you ensure that your actions are relevant. You could say something like this, "I want to replace your sweater. Would you like me to buy it for you, give you the money or get you a gift card?" In more complicated situations, I urge you to think long and hard before choosing to ask the person what they want you to do to make things right. While asking someone what they want you to do demonstrates a desire to rectify the situation, it can also be perceived as a willingness to do anything they ask. Before you open that door, know that if you refuse to follow through or take too long to follow through, you will only have made things worse.

Timing is another important thing to consider when it comes to making reparation. Making reparation as soon as possible communicates a sense of urgency and gives weight and value to your apology. This reminds me of an old saying that I believe to be very true, "Actions speak louder than words". I also believe, "Actions speak *longer* than words". What you do after apologizing matters more than the apology itself. As I mentioned before, after you apologize, you have the opportunity to live out your apology with your actions. If you follow the first two steps and promise that you will never do something again, but fail to keep that promise, you will not only lose credibility, but your words will also become more offensive. Remember, what you do matters more than what you say.

I want to offer a word to the wise recipient of an apology. The idea that a promise is comfort to a fool rings true if the word of the person making the promise can't be trusted. If someone makes a promise and breaks it again and again, it makes sense not to trust them. Even if you choose to forgive, that doesn't suddenly empower them to make different choices. If they are sincere, they will commit to a different course of action. The strong message of not letting yourself or others off the hook that I will repeat again and again is all about accountability. A Genuine Apology incorporates commitment but will also feature accountability.

Just like the Genuine Apology that Jonathan is building for Maggie, a healthy, mature and strong relationship will have accountability woven into it. Accountability occurs when two people agree that support will be offered to see a commitment through to its end, especially when it gets hard. Accountability is not the solution to undesirable behavior. It is a supportive element for the person who desires, and chooses, to change their behavior. The person's choice to change is integral to accountability. You cannot support someone to make changes that they don't choose to make. Yet, in addition to their choice, a plan is also integral to accountability. You cannot support someone to be faithful to a plan if they don't have one. Similarly, supporting someone to remain committed to a course of action that is unclear is also next to impossible.

It may sound like I am making something simple more complicated than it needs to be, however, most people find themselves breaking promises for one simple reason, saying what you will not do, is very different than saying what you will do. Saying what you will do involves identifying specific actions that you will take. Saying that you will never be unfaithful is very different than saying you will cut off contact with someone, share passwords and texts to rebuild trust and choose to come home consistently as opposed to stopping off for a drink after work.

Many people make well-intended promises and fail to keep them. Remember, if a particular offence happens continuously, the credibility of the person apologizing will be diminished until all trust is gone. Even if the promise seems simple to keep, I urge you to come up with a plan. From the cases I have witnessed, the promises people make seem easy enough to keep, yet they fail to follow through. In many situations, the missing piece of this puzzle is a well-thought-out plan. Let's think about this logically. If you've done something once, the chances are, it is possible and maybe even likely for it to happen again. The best way to avoid this is to understand the multiple factors that contributed to it happening and putting a plan in place to address those factors when they arise because they will return, they always do!

Make Your Plan Realistic

It is also important that the plan be realistic. What's the difference between a realistic plan and an unrealistic plan? For starters, a realistic plan is possible. Saying that you will never forget to do something again in life is not a realistic plan. Taking immediate action to define and implement strategies that are within your control to help you remember to do a particular thing will move you closer to having a realistic plan. Coming up with a realistic plan takes time. Trust, credibility and even the very existence of your relationship can hinge on your ability to follow through on the commitments you make, so it is worth taking the time to plan out what you will do and what it will take to follow through.

Again, a simple apology with a promise is often not enough. The many broken promises I hear about are proof enough that most people don't take the necessary time to make a plan that will help them avoid making the same choices. Plans that lack sufficient thought will crumble in the face of routine. Old patterns die hard, especially when they are supported by old friends who want to keep them alive. Those old friends might be people, but they could also be memories, values or beliefs. So, be prepared to stand your ground. Arm yourself with a well-laid out plan to help you keep your word. If you are sincere about another person's healing you will see the apology through to the end, even if it means enduring the discomfort of internal or interpersonal conflict.

The committed road of the Genuine Apology can also mean enduring the guilt and even sorrow of breaking promises to people outside of the significant relationship you are attempting to heal. The fact that a commitment to change also means reprioritizing is regularly overlooked. Sometimes that involves placing people above things, like golf, TV or work. Other times, it means prioritizing one relationship over another, like a family member over a friend or vice versa.

For those of you who decide to make a realistic plan, ensure that this plan does not invite the other person to be responsible for the execution of your plan, like the apology add-on discussed in chapter 2. You and your credibility will benefit the most from a plan that you can carry out without relying on someone else. I am well aware of this fact and have a story to prove it.

 Changing My Ways

My lovely wife, Adene, expressed her fear of my "assertive" driving on several occasions throughout the first few years of our marriage. I acknowledged her fear on several occasions, but didn't change my driving. As the years went by, she continued to express her discomfort, with an added level of anger, I might add, so I lovingly asked her to let me know when she was afraid, because her feelings mattered to me. I thought this was a great plan, because I was genuinely impacted by her feeling afraid, but the plan failed for two reasons. Reason number one, the plan was unrealistic! She was afraid. When people experience intense and unpleasant emotions, we don't readily access our logical thinking, so expecting her to calmly remind me about what I was doing when she was afraid was not a realistic plan. Secondly, the plan was unfair. By asking her to tell me when she was afraid, I was placing the responsibility on her to bring about change in my behavior. When you think of a plan, be sure to think of a plan that you can carry out without the other person reminding you.

Back to my insufficient plan for change. A couple more years went by without any lasting signs of progress. The maternal instinct to protect our newborn kicked my wife's fear and anger into high gear to the point of her considering separation. Yes, I, the family counsellor was blind to the pain I was causing my wife for years. The very real threat of my marriage ending and my family being separated catapulted my plan into a whole new realistic dimension.

My wife's clear expression of reaching the end of her rope with this issue, and possibly with me, helped me to appreciate that saying sorry wasn't good enough. I can remember so clearly, stopping myself from apologizing once again, sitting there with her at the kitchen table in silence. I recognized that I didn't know what to do. It literally took about 30 minutes of trying to figure out what I could do to change my driving. I feel compelled and honored to credit God with the following strategy because

I have no idea of where it came from. It just crystallized instantaneously in my mind. My new and improved plan looked like this, each time we got into the car I would say the following words out loud, "We are going to have a nice and safe ride today." I asked Adene to simply bear with me, because this was a strategic yet heart-felt part of my plan. While her fears always mattered to me, I needed to remember this before I started driving.

Communicating the details and meaning attached to my plan with Adene was essential because these words could easily be interpreted as belittling her and minimizing her concerns. Thankfully, she was willing to go along with my plan. After a couple of weeks, I began saying my reminder silently, to myself. After a while, I wasn't saying my "fear-free" driving statement anymore.

The new and improved plan worked because it was realistic and dependent upon me. It was also very thorough. Adding specific behaviors that I could implement immediately and repeat regularly in order to create a new routine helped me to make lasting change, but it was also the key to cultivating my wife's confidence in me. I admit, it wasn't just my efforts, Adene's presence in the car was also a visual reminder of the need for my new way of driving.

Step 3 - Verbalize your commitment
to a plan of Action

There are many strategies one can employ to remember things that are important. I will list a few at the end of this chapter, but in the meantime, I want to encourage you not to rely solely on your memory or good intentions. Be proactive and get prepared because familiar challenges will crop up again and again. Please don't wait until you are midway through committing the offence to try and make a change. Again, I know from personal experience, that doesn't work out too well. Make a plan as soon as you can. It may take an hour or a day to come up with a good plan, but that's ok. In fact, I have developed a workshop centred on making realistic plans for change, not just because it's difficult to do, but because it further demonstrates how serious one is about the commitment they are making.

After making a great plan, you will actually have something to commit to. Sharing this plan with the people that you love and have hurt is where a deeper level of trust, hope and expectation is cultivated. The relief that people experience when they hear about a plan is an amazing thing to witness. Your commitment to a plan, a good, realistic and well-thought-out plan, matters! Without a plan, all you have is a promise and that might not be enough over time.

A point of caution: Even with a good plan, there are times we may fall back into old patterns. The reality is, as I have said many times throughout this book, we are not perfect. In my case, during occasional moments of stress or anxiety, I tend to revert to my "assertive" driving style. And, yes, I may get a loving reminder from my wife, however, because of the specifics of my plan, it doesn't take me long to regroup and return to my new and improved style of driving. In addition to the blessing of Adene's forgiveness and understanding toward my flaws, my degree of success and demonstrated commitment to change over the years helps her to appreciate the challenges of old habits popping up every now and then.

It is also important to note that if Adene were not as understanding I could have become discouraged and chose to surrender to the old way of driving or simply let her drive. However, the choice to let discouragement or frustration stop me from making loving changes would have more to do with my maturity and my resolve to be the best husband that I can be than with her level of understanding. Having a clear sense of your motivation will help you see the value attached to your choice for change, which will help you stick to your plan.

Even though I've shared examples of an apology with reparation and one with a realistic plan, let's bring this chapter to a close by returning to Jonathan and Maggie's story. Again, we'll go back to step 1 then move forward to step 3 and focus on how Jonathan developed and verbalized a plan of action that he could commit to.

As you may recall, Jonathan took a deep breath and made another attempt.

(Step 1) "Maggie, I want to apologize for not telling you the day that I was let go, or at least the day after the shock had worn off.

(Step 2) "I will never forget the day I found you in front of the computer, crying. You looked stunned and heartbroken. If I were you I would have been so hurt and angry. I imagine you probably felt all of those feelings and more... I realize that I broke your heart when I broke your trust.

(Step 3) "If you will allow me to rebuild that trust I promise to never lie to you again."

"Jonathan", I quickly chimed in, "while you may be successful in keeping that promise, I encourage people to stay away from absolutes. Is there a specific course of action that addresses rebuilding trust in this situation in a very practical way that you can demonstrate immediately?"

"Yeah, of course. I already told Cynthia that I don't want more than a friendship with her, but I am willing to discontinue communication with her altogether if that will help." Maggie, nodded silently with an expression on her face that screamed, Well duh! Jonathan wisely replied,

"I won't contact her again. In fact, I will delete her contact information right now!" And he pulled out his phone and did just that.

I am aware that long after a fire has been put out, embers can continue to burn, reigniting a flame when you least expect it. So, I asked, "What will you do if she contacts you, even though you've ceased communication?"

"Andrew, I really don't think she will."

"She may not, but for sake of developing a solid plan that will help Maggie be clear about what you are committing to, what will you do if she does?"

"Well, I can let her know that even though she may simply want to continue a friendship with me I am choosing to discontinue communication with her in order to rebuild trust in my relationship with Maggie and ask that she not contact me again. Maggie, I can also show you the email or text and tell you about it if she calls. You already have my passwords... Is there anything else that I can do?" Moved with relief and growing confidence, Maggie appreciatively replied,

"Not that I can think of at the moment, Jon."

For your consideration

As noted above, a good plan requires thought and will help you to be proactive. Creating statements and even new routines can be very helpful. You can also use written reminders, memorize statements, post them in strategic places as well as use technology to help yourself remember.

Each plan will look different so if there are changes you want to commit to, take a moment to figure out what will help you to make those changes. You have the ability to change your life and your relationships, so why not do it now? You are about to approach the final step in building a Genuine Apology, but before you turn the page, are there changes you want to commit to? If so, what are they? Is your plan realistic and clear?

CHAPTER FOURTEEN

Step 4
Extend an Invitation

Step 1 provides the opportunity to demonstrate humility and take responsibility by labeling specific hurtful choices we've made. Step 2 exercises empathy as we imagine the impact of our actions. Step 3 allows us to enter into accountability by verbalizing a specific plan that we will commit to as well as making reparation where possible. So, here we are at the final step in building and offering a Genuine Apology. If you thought step 1 was difficult, brace yourself, because we have come to the most vulnerable part of offering a Genuine Apology, step 4 - Extending an invitation. To return to the bridge metaphor for a moment, steps 1-3 have helped you to build a strong bridge. You may have even consulted the hurt party about the specifications and bridge design, but now it is time to invite that person to take a step onto the bridge. This step is critical, for both of you.

It is important to ask the person if they have

anything they'd like to say to you. This is by far the most sensitive and vulnerable step in the process, because you cannot guarantee how they will respond. You may even be expecting an apology in return only to have the person say absolutely nothing or totally reject your apology. Because you cannot guarantee what the person will say or do, as I have said multiple times it is important to clarify and review your intentions before beginning to build and share your Genuine Apology.

As discussed in chapter 2, one of the keys to offering a meaning-full apology is focusing your intentions on bringing healing to the hurt you believe you have caused. The same applies to offering a Genuine Apology. If this is truly your intention, even if the other person's response doesn't fit your desired outcome, you can still feel content in knowing that you've done your part to try to make things better.

In all of the cases where I have coached either one or both people around giving and receiving Genuine Apologies, immediate acceptance of the apology and appreciation for the time and care that was given to it were expressed. All except one. In this situation, the person made a valiant attempt at offering an apology because she felt obligated and pressured to do so, but to her dismay and the disappointment of the person who desired a Genuine Apology, she was simply not ready to deliver one.

Although that was many years ago, the lesson I learned in that moment remains true, discerning your readiness for offering a Genuine Apology is key. While offering your apology is often part of your own healing, it is important to be healed enough before offering your Genuine Apology. This brings us back to the discussion in chapter 7 about forgiveness. I trust that it is clear that forgiveness will always precede reconciliation, but in situations where parties have hurt each other, forgiveness must also be given by the person offering the Genuine Apology before the apology is offered. Sometimes forgiving the person you are apologizing to is exactly what will help you to apologize without reservation.

In all my years of coaching and witnessing Genuine Apologies, when given without reservation, apologies were given in return. This is the response that we all hope for when offering sincere apologies but don't often receive. I believe that the limited number of returned apologies is due to the poor execution of apologies in the first place. If the guidelines we have discussed throughout this book are not observed and a few of the steps are missing, I'd say it's unrealistic to expect an apology in return, regardless of how sincere you are.

While we are on the topic of expectations, remembering that there is a difference between a desire and an expectation is invaluable. There is nothing wrong with desiring an apology in return, however, expecting one will put you in a different frame of mind, leading you to feel resentful if your expectation is not met. I want to remind you that even if you take the time to offer a Genuine Apology and observe all of the steps, the other person may not apologize right away and you may feel disappointed. Although Jonathan was desirous of Maggie being receptive of his apology, it was important for him to accept that he might not get one in return. Let's resume their story to see how she responded to his apology and if he received one in kind. Just to remind you of the values Jonathan, and eventually you, will experience and incorporate into your Genuine Apology, I have noted them as they appear in each step.

Jonathan took a deep breath and made another attempt.

(Step 1 – Humility and Responsibility) "Maggie, I want to apologize for not telling you the day that I was let go, or at least the day after the shock had worn off.

(Step 2 - Empathy) "I will never forget the day I found you in front of the computer, crying... I realize that I broke your heart when I broke your trust.

217

(Step 3 - Accountability) "I will delete Cynthia's contact information... and ask that she not contact me again. I will also show you the email or text and tell you about it if she calls.

(Step 4 - Vulnerability) "Maggie, I really hope you will forgive me and accept my apology. Please let me know if there is something else that I can do. I want to know what you're thinking."

Maggie paused and looked away, then turned to Jonathan again. Through tears, that Jonathan had not seen since that day she cried at the computer, Maggie professed, "Having the time to think about all that has happened helped me to realize that I took many things for granted over the years. I assumed that I would always know what you were thinking and feeling. It pains me, deeply, to know that you were feeling stressed and even depressed for months and I had no idea. Jon, I do accept your apology and I need to apologize to you, for not paying enough attention and asking about what was going in your life."

Jonathan couldn't contain himself anymore and began to cry. "Maggie, thank you for caring for me. I really needed to hear that. I accept your apology".

As much as Jonathan wanted his pain to be acknowledged, he couldn't ask for it. Thankfully, he didn't have to. Because he incorporated the values we discussed as he built an amazing bridge, Maggie was able to cross over. Let's take a walk through the steps that will help him *L.I.V.E.* out his Genuine Apology. 1) He *L*abeled the specific actions he was taking responsibility for. 2) He *I*magined and expressed how Maggie might have been impacted. 3) He *V*erbalized his commitment to a plan of action that he welcomed accountability for. 4) He *E*xtended an invitation for Maggie to share her thoughts.

Although humility was only noted in the parentheses of the first step, the truth is, it was embodied in his approach and permeated his entire apology. Maggie's response is evidence of her love for Jonathan as well as the effectiveness of his Genuine Apology. Now, that the healing has begun they are in the perfect position to forge the road ahead, together, and experience reconciliation.

As you prepare to take these steps, out of this book into your relationships, I want you to be prepared. So, be sure to reflect on the thoughts below.

For your consideration :

What To Expect When Taking Step 4
While this may be the most vulnerable part of

the apology for the person offering the apology, in all likelihood, this invitation will be unexpected and perhaps even awkward for the person receiving it. The hope is that, although it may be new, it will be a positive experience.

If this is a new concept and endeavour for you, here are some reactions to a Genuine Apology that you might encounter. Sometimes people will wait until you're finished and will offer some clarity about what was most hurtful about the situation or help you to understand more accurately what they've been feeling or thinking. They might also add to the list of offences and expect more apologies. If you receive any of the responses above, believe it or not, you've done a good job and you're on your way to restoring health in your relationship.

If you are caught off guard or upset by their reaction, as opposed to automatically apologizing or ruining all of your hard work by losing your temper, remember that you can buy time to give thought to what they've shared by saying something like, "Is it alright if we slow down, so that we can deal with one issue at a time?" Or, "I am a little caught off guard, I wasn't expecting you to say that."

If you're still feeling unsure about what to say in a moment like this, feel free to revisit some of the wording for taking time in chapter 3. If and when you do take time to gather your thoughts, you can replay the conversation and see if you agree with them. Search for things you can take responsibility for and then apologize where appropriate.

What Do You Do If Someone Doesn't Offer An Apology In Return?

In Jonathan's case, his apology was not only met with acceptance but it was reciprocated. Yet, what do you do if you believe you are owed an apology and don't receive one? After offering your Genuine Apology, give it some time. Some people might need time to process what you've shared and may return a short time afterwards with an apology. I don't advise asking for an apology.

Yes, I am aware that hurtful situations are rarely the result of one person's actions, however, if you desire an apology in return, asking for one in that moment can cast a shadow on your apology, moving the other person to question your intentions and your sincerity. Telling someone that he/she owes you an apology is an option, however, very rarely does someone respond well if you demand an apology, especially if you have hurt them. An hour later, a day later or a week later your longed-for apology just might arrive, so don't let your desire for an immediate apology dictate your behavior and rob you of something that you value.

If a couple days go by and a well-deserved apology doesn't seem to be coming, asking the person if they are aware of how their actions impacted you or if they'd be open to hearing what was upsetting for you are also options to consider. These approaches are less likely to bring the sincerity of your apology into question but also give you an opportunity to share your perspective about the situation without accusing the person or blaming them. You are simply inviting the other person to reflect on what they can take responsibility for.

If someone is unable or unwilling to take responsibility for their actions, then you are left with choices to make about what kind of relationship you want to be in with this person moving forward. This brings us back to the topic of reconciliation. If someone refuses to change, regardless of their reason(s), it speaks to their readiness for relationship with you. Reconciliation involves gaining clarity and agreement on the road ahead in order to walk forward together. You play an important role in deciding on the quality and closeness of the relationships you are in and how you want things to progress. The reality is, the role the other person plays is just as important. You may want to apologize and be reconciled, but the other person might not give you the chance. Whether we are talking about someone giving you an apology or receiving one from you, there is a chance that you may be hurt and disappointed by their response, but remember your intentions for offering the apology in the first place.

Perhaps you picked up this book because of unresolved and unaddressed hurts that have been around for far too long or some caring soul gave it to you because they are tired of seeing you in pain. If you've been considering offering a Genuine Apology to someone you care about, it's important to acknowledge that the events and feelings that lead to what you've been thinking of are not likely to go away on their own. You have the option to continue to endure the undercurrents of resentment and eruptions of dormant anger or take the chance to pursue the peace that I believe you desire.

Even though there will always be the risk of disappointment, the truth is, you will never experience the healing of your significant relationships if you don't muster up the courage to try. That's the reason why I wrote this book. I wanted to try. I had to try, not just to change my relationships, or those of the people that I get to work with, but to change ideas and beliefs about apologies for everyone, everywhere. As I said, while I don't believe we always hurt the ones we love, I know that hurting them and being hurt by them is inevitable.

We will experience multiple hurts and have multiple conversations about those hurts, so why not make them fruitful? Can you imagine what would happen in our world if everyone chose to care enough to learn how to address the hurts they've caused to the people closest to them?

I am confident that the content of this book will change the course of many relationships and help people to experience healing in their most significant relationships, however, the choice to try is and always will be yours.

CHAPTER FIFTEEN

My Invitation to You

Some people will read or hear the kind of dialogue between Jonathan and Maggie and think to themselves, *"Nobody talks like that!"* Fortunately, that train of thought is wrong. What I would agree with is that very few people are taught to communicate like this. It's easy for me to believe people can communicate this way, based on the fact that people do, when the conversation makes room for them to.

Even though this scenario was not based on a real couple, elements of this story can be seen in many families around the world. Taking things for granted, staying silent when it is best to speak, turning away from each other instead of turning towards each other, speaking to anyone and everyone except the person we have the issue with, shutting out the truth when it is best to listen keenly for it. More to the specifics of this book, shirking responsibility, being self-focused and dismissing accountability in order to stay in control and avoid feeling vulnerable is what too many people do.

Nobody enjoys feeling vulnerable and out of control, but observing the guidelines and steps shared in this book will help you to slow the pace of your interactions, give thought to what you're feeling, thinking and what you actually want to say. When you take the time to adopt and use these strategies, you will find yourself thinking, feeling and speaking differently. Yes, it takes time and practice, but so does ruining apologies and returning to important conversations in the same old way. I hope this is something you want to change.

I was told that practice makes perfect, however, I have ceased my pursuit of perfection and simply seek to improve every day. Most people have the capacity to do what this book suggests, but the question is, will you demonstrate the consistent commitment to take these steps over and over again until they become natural. If longstanding change is what you want then I recommend that you be consistent and practice, practice, practice. It's the best way to make and sustain change.

If you are dissatisfied with the way you apologize or the apologies others have given to you, I hope you have recognized some practical ways to bring about change in those interactions. I also hope that you will be brave enough to actually use these steps to address past, current and future hurts in your most significant relationships. If you've been telling yourself it's too late for apologies, I want to remind you that death is the only unmovable barrier to offering or receiving a Genuine Apology, so don't wait until it's too late.

If you're open to it and remain consistent with the strategies you've learned here, you will become an example of someone who knows how to offer a Genuinely Apology. You will also be someone who can deal with conflict and manage your emotions well, too!

Finally, I am aware that it is impossible for one book to address everything, so I want to know what I have missed and what you'd like more discussion about. I would also love to hear about your experiences with using the techniques and tips in this book as you bring healing to your most significant relationships. I wish you the best and feel free to get in touch with me through my website, www.coachdrew.ca.

I look forward to hearing from you,

Andrew L. Blackwood

About the Author

Andrew L. Blackwood is a native to Toronto, Canada and currently lives in Brampton with his wonderful wife and two precious daughters. His love for writing finds its most frequent expression in his journaling, a highly prized spiritual discipline that feeds his soul and clears his mind. His education at Tyndale Seminary in Toronto *(Master of Divinity in Counselling)* and Palmer's Theological Seminary of Eastern University in Philadelphia *(Doctor of Ministry to Marriage and Family)* enables him to blend Family Systems Theories, Cognitive Behavioral Therapy, Experiential Therapy, Narrative Therapy and his faith together in a way that is personal to him yet respectful to whoever he has the opportunity to meet.

When Andrew isn't Consulting, Coaching/Counselling clients or facilitating workshops he is actively mentoring youth, speaking and making use of his first degree in music as he leads worship at his church, Dayspring Christian Church in Brampton.

Made in the USA
Las Vegas, NV
18 November 2022